Over 100 delicious recipes for effortless
weight loss & vibrant health

THE PRIMAL
BLUEPRINT

QUICK & EASY
COOKBOOK

MARK SISSON

10 9 8 7 6 5 4 3 2 1

First published in the United Kingdom in 2014 by Vermilion, an imprint of Ebury Publishing
A Random House Group company
First published in the United States of America by Primal Nutrition, Inc. in 2011

The Random House Group Limited Reg. No. 954009

Addresses for companies within the Random House Group can be found at
www.randomhouse.co.uk

The Random House Group Limited supports the Forest Stewardship Council® (FSC®), the leading
international forest-certification organisation. Our books carrying the FSC label are printed on
FSC® -certified paper. FSC is the only forest-certification scheme supported by the leading
environmental organisations, including Greenpeace. Our paper procurement policy can be found
at www.randomhouse.co.uk/environment

Printed and bound in China by C&C Offset Printing Co., Ltd

ISBN 9780091954987

To buy books by your favourite authors and register for offers visit www.randomhouse.co.uk

The information in this book has been compiled by way of general guidance in relation to the specific subjects addressed, but is not a substitute and not to be relied on for medical, healthcare, pharmaceutical or other professional advice on specific circumstances and in specific locations. So far as the author is aware the information given is correct and up to date as at April 2014. Practice, laws and regulations all change, and the reader should obtain up to date professional advice on any such issues. The author and publishers disclaim, as far as the law allows, any liability arising directly or indirectly from the use, or misuse, of the information contained in this book.

ACKNOWLEDGMENTS

Mark Sisson

I must acknowledge first and foremost all my wonderful readers over at my ever-expanding blog MarksDailyApple.com. Their enthusiasm and support have helped raise awareness of the Primal Blueprint lifestyle to the point where it is poised to become a mainstream phenomenon. Reader questions, suggestions and directions have also helped guide these most recent Primal culinary explorations. I like the way you guys think.

My co-author Jennifer Meier has once again exceeded expectations in bringing to life a wide variety of brand new delicious, yet easy-to-prepare, meals. I must confess that many of these were initially designed to appeal to my own finicky palate and my relative impatience in the kitchen (I want fabulous food and I want it now), so the challenge was double. Most of her work was done while pregnant with her first child, and once again Jennifer did double duty as the food photographer. Talk about multitasking!

I also want to thank Aaron Fox, my general manager and webmaster of MarksDailyApple.com, who was instrumental in coordinating the efforts of everyone involved in this project, served as the main copy editor and handled the indexing. MarksDailyApple.com staffers Bradford Hodgson and Cailyn Roybal added valuable insights and fact checking, with Cailyn assuming the task of divining all the macronutrient breakdowns. My super designer Kristin Roybal came through (again) with a fabulous design and layout of both the text and cover.

Special thanks to my beautiful wife, Carrie, and fabulous children, Devyn and Kyle, for their love and support as we all look to see what the Primal Blueprint holds for the future.

Jennifer Meier

Thank you Mark Sisson and Aaron Fox for introducing me to the world of Primal eating and for being so enthusiastic about creating the best recipes possible. A huge thank you to the online community at MarksDailyApple.com—your insatiable appetite for great food has inspired all the recipes in this cookbook. And thanks, of course, to my husband, Sorin, who happily eats everything I cook.

TABLE OF CONTENTS

94 Dinner

INTRODUCTION

PEOPLE ARE THINKING ABOUT FOOD MORE THAN EVER. What we eat, where and how it was grown or raised, and the endless ways in which it can be prepared all continue to be hot topics of conversation. The primal eating pattern of our hunter-gatherer ancestors – consuming a wide range of fresh, organic, seasonal foods – is being celebrated in modern times. And yet, simultaneously, obesity rates and lifestyle diseases continue to be on the rise. Our society continues to be dependent on processed foods and addicted to sugars, grains and man-made fats that our bodies are not genetically programmed to thrive on.

So many of us have made the connection that eating well brings pleasure, and that what we eat directly affects how we feel. Yet, we cannot fully break free from the foods and lifestyle habits that are causing us harm.

The solution to this modern dilemma does not have to be complicated. Nor does it have to involve the deprivation we've been led to believe is necessary. Ten simple, logical steps that served our primal ancestors well not just for surviving, but for genetically thriving, can continue to serve us well in the modern world: Eat lots of plants and animals. Move around at a slow pace. Lift heavy things. Run really fast every once in awhile. Get lots of sleep. Play. Get some sunlight every day. Avoid trauma. Avoid poisonous things. Use your mind.

It's that simple. Or is it? The frenetic pace of modern existence can seem at odds with these core beliefs of the Primal Blueprint. How can we possibly enjoy a happy, healthy, balanced lifestyle while living in such a hectic world?

Here's the thing: the Primal Blueprint gives you immense personal power to make necessary changes in your life with minimal sacrifice and little chance of failure. Every Primal law doesn't have to be followed every day; rather, it's about incorporating them over time into a longer journey; a journey that leads to overall physical and mental well-being. And what better way to begin that journey than by sitting down to a delicious home cooked meal?

For the uninitiated, the Primal Blueprint eating strategy simply seeks to emulate the hunter-gatherer diet of our ancestors (find out more in my best-selling book *The Primal Blueprint*). Our primary goals are the elimination of most simple sugars, grains (wheat, rye, barley, corn, etc.), legumes (soya, kidney beans, etc.) and trans and hydrogenated fats and oils—foods that our genes never encountered until very recently in human history. Moreover, these are often the same foods that confuse our genes into making us sick over a long period of time. Instead, the Primal Blueprint focuses on quality cuts of meat, fish, fowl, eggs, copious amounts of vegetables, fruits, and healthy, life-sustaining fats. These are the foods our genes expect us to be eating and which promote a healthy weight, abundant energy, and a robust immune system.

Primal Blueprint Quick & Easy Meals contains 110 recipes that are completely Primal and will simultaneously meet all the needs of anyone seeking a gluten-free, low carb, low dairy, or paleo existence. And here's the best part: every recipe is written specifically with your busy lifestyle in mind. Delicious, easy-to-prepare recipes like Chorizo and Almond Crusted Halibut and Tahini Chicken Salad are proof that 'convenience food' does not have to be pre-packaged and processed. In 30 minutes or less you can have healthy, satisfying and unbelievably flavourful meals on the table that you can feel good about.

And with the handy macronutrient profiles (courtesy of the very useful site FitDay.com) included with each recipe you'll know exactly what you're putting in your body, no guesswork required. Each profile is per serving, with per serving figures calculated based on the upper recipe serving size. For example, if the recipe creates 2–4 servings, the per serving macronutrient profile will be based on a 4 serving recipe (i.e. fat, carb, protein quantities divided by 4, not 2). Likewise, for recipes that call for a range of an individual ingredient, the upper ingredient quantity is used when determining the macronutrient profile. For example, if a recipe calls for 675–900 g (1½ to 2 lb) of chicken, 900 g (2 lb) of chicken were used when calculating the profile. Keep in mind that all calculations are approximations, and that figures have been rounded to the nearest whole number. As such, aggregate totals may not amount to the expected value in some cases. While all meals in this cookbook have a place in a Primal diet, armed with this knowledge you'll be equipped to pick and choose recipes depending on your own personal weight loss or weight maintenance goals.

You'll also find helpful hints, easy-to-follow instructions and colour photos on each page, making your time in the kitchen (even if it's only 30 minutes!) less stressful and more fun. What you won't find in this book are low-fat, low-flavour 'diet' foods or ingredients like grains, trans and hydrogenated fats and excessive sugars and dairy. Instead, dishes like Pork and Shiitake Lettuce Cups and Espresso Rubbed Steak will bring new flavours and variety to your table, proving once again that eating Primal is about expanding your culinary horizons, not limiting them.

PRIMAL BLUEPRINT LAW #1: EAT LOTS OF PLANTS AND ANIMALS

BECAUSE OUR PRIMAL ANCESTORS HAD NO OTHER OPTION, they ate a diet that varied widely and consisted only of what they could catch or forage: meat, fowl and seafood, fruits and vegetables, tubers, nuts and seeds. Without knowing it, they were also ingesting antioxidants, polyphenols, minerals, healthy fats and protein – nutrients our bodies need now more than ever to thrive.

In the 21st century we have plenty of options – too many one could argue – leading us away from the simple but well-balanced and nourishing Primal diet that suited our species so well for so long. What we don't have, however, is the time to spend all day hunting and gathering and preparing our meals.

Primal Blueprint Quick & Easy Meals makes it more convenient than ever to eat the foods you should be eating with very little hassle. This cookbook will make transitioning to the Primal Blueprint eating style simple, and can help those who have already committed to Primal eating stay on track.

BREAKFAST, LUNCH AND DINNER

WHETHER WE LIKE IT OR NOT, MODERN LIFE USUALLY REVOLVES AROUND A SCHEDULE. Getting to work on time, getting the kids to football practice, getting dinner on the table by a certain hour... you're probably all too familiar with the routine.

Our ancient ancestors didn't punch a time clock every day and they probably didn't eat dinner every night at exactly 6 pm. They ate when they were hungry or when food was available. For over two million years of human history, this random, sporadic, intermittent eating pattern shaped our DNA. Today we work with the very same genetic recipe and, as a result, our bodies are well-equipped to deal with both grazing and intermittent eating. Allowing for these variations in eating patterns makes following an eating plan less stressful and frees you to respond to genuine hunger, not a ticking clock.

Still, regular meal times remind us to set aside a piece of the day to nourish ourselves and take a necessary break. For ease of use, the recipes in *Primal Blueprint Quick & Easy Meals* are divided into universal meal categories: breakfast, lunch, dinner, and snacks/starters (with some flavourful sauces and spice rubs thrown in at the end). Don't let these categories restrict how you use this cookbook. There's nothing wrong with a Fennel and

Olive Omelette for dinner and Pork Fried Cauliflower Rice for breakfast if that's what you crave. Better yet, double the recipes you cook so you can eat them for dinner one night and as a snack the next day.

However you use this cookbook and whenever you eat your meals, remember that just because you're cooking quickly doesn't mean you have to eat quickly. Spending less time in the kitchen gives you more time to sit and enjoy the meal. Take time to appreciate the food you've just cooked and enjoy the calories that are fuelling your body. Eating mindfully also helps sustain long-term health and fitness goals by making you more aware of how much and what you're eating.

SHOPPING STRATEGIES AND COOKING SHORT-CUTS

PREPARING A GREAT MEAL IN 30 MINUTES OR LESS CAN TAKE A LITTLE PRACTICE. If you don't cook often, you may find that a few of the recipes in this cookbook will take you longer to make than we've predicted. The first time, anyway. The more you cook, the faster and more skilled you'll become. You'll become comfortable using the recipes as a guide, then ad-libbing a little bit as you go, adding a little more of this and a little less of that to suit your own palate.

If you're someone who has no trouble getting a meal on the table in 30 minutes or less, this cookbook will inspire you to branch out and experiment with new ingredients and cooking techniques. It's easy to get caught in a rut and fall back on the same tried-and-true, easy-to-get-on-the-table meals week after week. This not only gets boring, it also limits the variety of foods in your diet.

In either case, whether you're following the recipes in this cookbook or cooking free-style without any recipe at all, a well-stocked kitchen and a few simple cooking strategies make it much easier to throw together a Primal meal.

Keep Non-perishables Well-stocked

These ingredients are the building blocks for Primal meals and will keep for weeks or months if your store cupboards stay relatively dark and cool.

Quick & Easy Tip:

Visit **MarksDailyApple.com** to take advantage of hundreds of Primal cooking and lifestyle tips and to join the conversation about what it means to live Primally in the modern world.

Healthy Oils

With more and more types of cooking oil crowding the shelves at the supermarkets and more and more conflicting advice about each one, what should be a simple purchase suddenly feels very complicated. It doesn't have to be; we've analyzed and cooked with all of them for you. These are the oils to keep in your kitchen:

OLIVE OIL – When in doubt, olive oil is a safe bet for most of your cooking needs. Virgin or extra-virgin olive oil is what you want to buy, and although extra virgin is supposed to have superior flavour, this isn't always the case – what is superior flavour to one person is only so-so to another. Some people like delicate, hardly noticeable flavour and some love a peppery, fruity full-flavoured oil. Finding your personal favourite requires trying different brands. If you decide to splurge on a more-expensive olive oil or are lucky enough to have locally bottled oil, reserve it for drizzling on salads and already-cooked food, as heat can diminish its flavour.

COCONUT OIL – This oil has a special place in my Primal heart, and not only because it's such a fantastic source of the healthy saturated fat that is essential to so many of our bodily functions. Coconut oil is shelf stable, stands up to heat well and tastes delicious. Unrefined virgin oil is what you want, whether you're cooking with it or using it to moisturize your hair.

NUT OILS – As long as you avoid groundnut (peanut) oil (technically, it's a legume and shouldn't even be considered a nut oil) many others are worth trying in moderation. Two especially worth seeking out, both for flavour and health benefits, are walnut and macadamia. An occasional drizzle of these nut oils on a salad or already-cooked dish can add amazing flavour. Avoid heating nut oils or keeping them for more than six weeks, as they are prone to rancidity. You should keep nut oil in the refrigerator.

SESAME OIL – Sesame is another highly flavourful oil to keep in the store cupboard (or refrigerator), but not one to use daily. It stands up to heat fairly well and can be used for quick high-heat cooking, like stir-frying, or used to add a distinct flavour to sauces and dressings.

PALM OIL – Virgin red palm oil is the most nutrient-rich, although it has a distinct taste that can alter the flavour of food in a way some people don't enjoy. Nevertheless, it's chock full of vitamins and antioxidants and very shelf stable.

GHEE – Ghee is ultra-clarified butter, basically pure butterfat that has been relieved of all lactose and dairy proteins. It has a nutty, pleasant flavour and can be used in the exact same way as butter, with one highly convenient difference: ghee will keep for months without refrigeration.

Nuts

True, many nuts do have a high omega-6 content and over-indulgence could potentially tilt you towards pro-inflammatory bodily processes as we discuss in *The Primal Blueprint*, but this view of nuts is too simplistic. Overall, a nut is a pretty complete nutritional source and in moderation can add incomparable richness and texture to a dish. Best bets are almonds, macadamia nuts, hazelnuts, pecans, brazil nuts, pine nuts and pistachios.

Flour Alternatives

Those nuts in your store cupboard aren't just for snacking; they can also be ground up and used as a substitute for flour in many recipes. Nut flours do not have the same properties as wheat flour, however, so some experimentation is necessary. For baking, blanched nut flours (the skin is removed from the nut) typically work best. Un-blanched nut flours are commonly labelled as nut flours. Coconut flakes can also be ground into a flour-like consistency. Both nut and coconut flour are available in most health food shops. Both should be stored in airtight containers; if you're not using them up within a month or so, consider keeping these flours in the fridge.

SPICES

Spices are a great way to add new flavour to meat and give vegetables an entirely different personality. For maximum flavour, buy whole spices and grind them yourself. At the very least, replace pre-ground spices every six months.

Sea Vegetables

At least in the western world, sea vegetables (more commonly referred to as simply seaweed) are an often-overlooked nutritional powerhouse. Most varieties are sold dried and keep well for long periods of time.

Coconut Milk

Unsweetened, canned coconut milk can add richness and flavour to soups, sauces and baked goods and is ideal for simmering meats or vegetables. Coconut milk keeps for many months on the shelf, but should be refrigerated and used within a few days after opening.

Salt

In moderation, salt brings out tremendous flavour in foods and for most people can also have some health benefits. And the great thing about cooking at home is that you get to control exactly how much salt goes into your food. Unrefined and unprocessed sea salt, mineral salts and rock salts are loaded with minerals, and have a pure flavour – a little bit goes a long way. Varieties with larger flakes, such as fleur de sel, celtic grey salt and Himalayan Pink salt, are best used to season a dish after it's already been cooked.

Sweeteners

If you're craving a little sweetness or need it to balance the flavours in a dish, raw honey and pure maple syrup are good to have on hand. In small quantities, dried fruits without any added sugar can be used for the same reasons.

Buy the Freshest Perishables Possible

One of the most memorable meals I've had was also one of the simplest. I was travelling in Spain and was served a dinner of fresh fish seared quickly in high-quality, local olive oil. Perfectly Primal and perfectly delicious. There were no complex sauces or seasonings and yet, years later I can't get this meal out of my mind. Some of this can be attributed to the setting – I was taking time to relax and enjoy and truly taste each bite – but mostly it was the incredible freshness of the ingredients. The fish had probably been caught that day and the olive oil was pressed from olives grown nearby. Fresh, high-quality ingredients speak for themselves. You don't need to spend hours in the kitchen to make them taste good. If buying organic, grass-fed beef means you can't afford to eat as much beef as you once did, consider this is a wise trade-off. Cultured butter made from the milk of grass-fed cows and free-range organic eggs are investments that will pay off as well in terms of your overall well-being. Beyond being conscious of how your food is raised, knowing where it comes from matters, too. Buy locally from farmers' markets when you can, or grow your own. I guarantee you'll taste the difference.

Make Your Own Condiments, Sauces, Dressings and Stocks

Many bottled condiments, sauces and dressings are filled with undesirable sugars and preservatives. Canned stock is usually high in sodium and low on flavour. Plan ahead a little, and your refrigerator and freezer can be well-stocked with homemade versions of all these immensely useful perishables. Visit MarksDailyApple.com for recipes that will show you how to make everything from homemade ketchup and BBQ sauce to beef stock.

Join a Veg Box Scheme

If you can't get to a farmers' market to buy local produce each week, or if you find yourself buying the same three vegetables week after week at the supermarket, consider subscribing to a fruit and veg box scheme. These boxes come directly from local farmers and are filled with a variety of seasonal produce straight to your door.

Chop Vegetables Ahead of Time

How long have those unpeeled carrots and that head of kale been staring back at you from the refrigerator? Despite our best intentions, sometimes the thought of cleaning and prepping vegetables is enough to prevent us from eating them. Dedicating just a half hour or so each week to cleaning, peeling and chopping produce makes mealtime a snap. Store the produce in airtight containers and then throughout the week snack on the veggies or throw them into salads, stir-frys and omelettes. If you're really pressed for time, consider buying pre-cut vegetables at the supermarket. You'll be amazed by how quickly vegetables disappear when anyone – including kids – can easily grab a handful on the go. And if you have children, consider having them help do the prep. It's a great way to get them involved in a Primal eating style early in life.

Get To Know Your Butcher and Fishmonger

Most butchers and fishmongers, especially those you shop with regularly, are happy to prep proteins to your specifications. If a recipe calls for meat or seafood to be cut a certain way, have them do it for you. Buying a fish that's already been skinned and de-boned by a professional or an entire chicken that's been perfectly cut up can save you time and frustration later.

Cook Double Portions of Protein

The steak you had for dinner on Monday would be fantastic in a breakfast burrito on Tuesday morning, or in a steak salad on Wednesday. Cooking extra amounts of protein with the intention of eating it later in the week will make throwing together meals less of a hassle, especially when it comes to packing lunches.

Cook Double Portions of Everything

Any of the recipes in this cookbook can be doubled and stretched into more than one meal. Plan on eating the leftovers later in the week, or freeze some for further down the road. Freezing is a great solution if you're someone who doesn't want to be cooking every night of the week. Of course, this means you'll have to...

Invest In a Freezer

A good freezer will allow you to not only freeze cooked meals for later use, but also stay stocked up on vegetables and fruit year round. This can be especially valuable if you live in an area where the dark days of winter limit the types of fresh produce available. A freezer also makes fiscal sense by allowing large meat purchases – like buying a whole pig or cow from a farmer or taking advantage of sales at the butcher shop.

While the freezer that's connected to your fridge can hold small amounts of food for short periods of time, a deep freezer can hold large amounts of food. Lined freezerproof paper and sealed containers and bags made specifically for freezing are a necessary investment to protect the food from freezer burn. If you have the space, a chest freezer is the best choice, since the cold air stays in the freezer when you open it.

Take Advantage of Technology

Our Primal ancestors may have got along just fine with kitchen tools like sharpened rocks and sticks, but I'm willing to bet a food processor would have made their lives a lot easier. To make cooking less work, consider investing in some modern conveniences:

MICROWAVE – We're not suggesting you cook every meal in the microwave, but if using it now and then means you're eating healthy foods that you wouldn't normally bother with, then a microwave can come in handy. As you'll see in several recipes from this cookbook, food that normally takes a long time to cook – squash, root vegetables, aubergine – can be cooked quickly in a microwave without sacrificing flavour or texture.

FOOD PROCESSOR – If you cook often, this appliance will more than pay for itself. Food processors can grate, chop and purée just about anything and make nut butters, chop vegetables, mix sauces and even mince meat. Smaller models are available, but have limited usability. Consider buying one that holds at least 2.1 litres.

BLENDER/IMMERSION BLENDER – Smoothies are one of the fastest and easiest meals around, especially if you own a blender. Blenders are also great for puréeing soups and sauces.

PRESSURE COOKER – Whole chickens, roasts and stews, tender vegetables and stock: all of these things are possible in an hour or less with a pressure cooker. When you don't have time to braise food for hours in the oven, a pressure cooker comes to the rescue.

SLOW COOKER – So this won't actually get a meal on the table in record time (hence the name) but it will decrease the actual amount of time you spend cooking a meal. That's because a slow cooker does it all for you; all you have to do is get the ingredients in the pot.

FOOD DEHYDRATOR – While not an essential Primal cooking tool, this handy appliance makes creating delicious beef, venison or turkey jerkies and dried fruit a cinch.

Take Advantage of Low-tech Tools

Ask any chef and they will tell you that the only tool you really need is a sharp knife. As true as this is (especially the sharp part) most home cooks find that a few other tools make life easier in the kitchen. You don't need every gadget in the cooking store, far from it, but there are a few to consider:

KITCHEN SHEARS – Easier to use than a knife, you can cut fresh herbs and greens with kitchen shears, but will find them the most helpful when trimming meat and seafood.

SALAD SPINNER – Soggy lettuce loses its crisp texture and doesn't soak up the flavour of salad dressing as well. With a salad spinner, you can wash and dry lettuce in record time.

GARLIC PRESS – 'Finely chopped garlic' just might be the most frequent phrase written in all cookbooks. A garlic press does all the work for you.

A GOOD CHOPPING BOARD – Your chopping board should be large enough that food doesn't slide over the edges while you're prepping and stable enough that it doesn't rock back and forth and slide while you chop. Buy a large board that has traction on the bottom, or use this trick: place a slightly damp towel under your chopping board to keep it from sliding.

COOKING WITHOUT A RECIPE

EVEN THOUGH THIS IS A COOKBOOK, IT'S WORTH NOTING THAT EATING PRIMALLY DOESN'T ALWAYS MEAN FOLLOWING RECIPES. In fact, some of the Primal meals and snacks I turn to most often are so simple that I didn't even bother creating recipes for them. Once your kitchen is well-stocked with the wide range of foods available to you on the Primal diet, you'll find that putting together a Primal meal or snack can be as simple as getting creative with what you have on hand. What are some of my five-minute favourites?

THE BIG-ASS SALAD – Throw some lettuce in a bowl, add a handful of the veggies you've pre-chopped, top it up with a handful of nuts or some protein leftover from dinner the night before, toss with a generous dousing of oil and lemon... *voilà!* You've got yourself a Big-ass Salad. This salad often ends up being the biggest meal of my day.

STUFFED AVOCADOS – Think of an avocado as an edible bowl. Take out the stone and fill the hole it leaves with a mashed hard-boiled egg topped with crumbled bacon.

NUT BUTTER – True, you can buy pre-made nut butter, but you can also pulse some nuts in a food processor and get the same creamy result. Eat it by the spoonful or use nut butter as a dip for veggies and fruit, and occasionally with dark chocolate.

SMOOTHIES – Two or three scoops of **Primal Fuel**. Water. Ice. Blend. Done. If you have more time, you can get creative with your smoothies. Try one of these combos:

Coconut Milk, Frozen Berries
Coconut Milk, Almond Butter, Cocoa Powder
Coconut Milk, Cooked Squash (or canned pumpkin), Cinnamon
Coconut Water, Egg Yolk, Frozen Blueberries
Ice, Spinach, Avocado, Hot Sauce
Ice, Cucumber, Avocado, Tomato

SANDWICH WRAP – Spread out a Romaine or cos lettuce leaf and fill it with chopped leftover meat, tomatoes, avocado and a dollop of mayonnaise. Wrap the leaf around the filling.

SCRAMBLES – Whisk some eggs, throw 'em in a pan with butter and leftover meat and veggies. Good for breakfast, lunch and dinner!

COCONUT SOUP – Bring equal parts chicken stock and coconut milk to the boil. Add spinach and prawns. Simmer 2–3 minutes.

TRAIL MIX – Throw together a few handfuls of nuts with 80 g (3 oz) of dried cranberries or raisins, unsweetened coconut and a sprinkle of cinnamon.

When you don't have any time at all, these ready-to-eat foods can be Primal snack staples:

CANNED SARDINES AND SALMON

SMOKED SALMON

LEFTOVER COOKED MEAT

COLD PRAWNS

OLIVES

FULL-FAT GREEK YOGURT

FRESH BERRIES

FRESH VEGGIES DIPPED IN SALSA OR GUACAMOLE

NUTS AND NUT BUTTERS

JERKY

PORK RINDS

AVOCADOS

Quick & Easy Tip:

Primal Fuel is a high-protein, low-carb, moderate-fat, meal replacement powder made with mostly Primal ingredients – no HFCS, artificial sweeteners, soya, unhealthy fats, low-quality protein or any other ingredients that you usually find in meal replacements.

Whey protein is another option for adding protein to smoothies, and although it isn't strictly Primal, whey protein can be an effective, occasional high-protein meal replacement.

RECIPES

BREAKFAST

NUTTY BLUEBERRY PROTEIN BALLS

Time in the Kitchen: 15 minutes
Servings: 12 balls *(macronutrient profile based on serving size of 2)*

4   dates, stones removed

100 g (3½ oz) walnuts

75 g (2¾ oz) macadamia nuts

2   tablespoons coconut oil

75 g (2¾ oz) fresh or defrosted blueberries (fresh work best)

40 g (1½ oz) coconut flakes

These little balls of protein are packed with tons of healthy fat and are the perfect snack when you're on the run. They're also a healthy way to satisfy a sweet tooth. Change the flavour of Nutty Blueberry Protein Balls by using different types of nuts each time you make them. Other variations include adding cinnamon, dark chocolate, or dried fruit instead of fresh. Or, instead of coconut, roll the finished balls in sesame seeds.

Pulverize dates in a food processor until a paste forms, about 40 seconds (the paste will typically come together in a clump).

Add walnuts and macadamia nuts and blend until very finely chopped, about 35 seconds.

With the blade still running, drizzle in coconut oil and stop as soon as the oil is blended in. Scrape the batter into a bowl and stir in the blueberries and 20 g (¾ oz) of the coconut.

Form the batter into round balls, then roll in leftover coconut flakes. Pop a few in your mouth immediately, and refrigerate the rest for snacking later!

Macronutrient Profile (per serving)

	Grams	Calories	%-Cals
Calories		340	
Fat	29	243	71%
Saturated	9	76	22%
Polyunsaturated	10	82	24%
Monounsaturated	9	74	22%
Carbohydrate	22	82	24%
Dietary Fibre	4		
Protein	5	16	5%

BERRY CRUMBLE

Time in the Kitchen: 15 minutes
Servings: 3

55 g (2 oz) walnuts

75 g (2¾ oz) pecans

a pinch of salt

¼ teaspoon cinnamon

⅛ teaspoon cardamom or nutmeg

1 tablespoon butter, cut into small pieces

1 tablespoon vanilla

140 g (4½ oz) berries (frozen or fresh)

A berry crumble is usually something thought of as dessert, but when made without any flour, oats or added sugar, it becomes a perfectly Primal, high-antioxidant breakfast. The berries and nuts are delicious alone, but a drizzle of coconut milk or dollop of yogurt on top add to the 'yum' factor.

Preheat the grill to low.

In a food processor or blender, grind walnuts so they are very finely chopped. Add pecans, salt, cinnamon, cardamom and butter and pulse until just blended, 10–15 seconds.

In a small pot, heat berries with vanilla. Bring to a gentle boil for 5 minutes, so the berries are well heated.

Drain off any liquid the berries have released and spoon the berries into a small ovenproof dish.

Spoon the nut mixture evenly on top of berries. Put under the grill and heat for several minutes until the topping is lightly browned. Keep an eye on the crumble as it cooks; if the grill is too hot the nuts are bound to burn.

Macronutrient Profile (per serving)

	Grams	Calories	%-Cals
Calories		350	
Fat	30	255	73%
Saturated	5	41	12%
Polyunsaturated	14	115	33%
Monounsaturated	10	86	24%
Carbohydrate	17	65	19%
Dietary Fibre	6		
Protein	6	20	6%

Quick & Easy Tip:

If you buy a large bag of walnuts for this recipe, use the remaining nuts to make *Creamy Walnut Sauce* (page 196) or *Nutty Blueberry Protein Balls* (page 4).

BERRY PANCAKE

Time in the Kitchen: 25 minutes
Servings: 4

3 tablespoons unsalted butter

150 g (5 oz) berries

4 large eggs, separated into whites and yolks

1 teaspoon vanilla extract

½ teaspoon cinnamon

This giant pancake has a texture between a soufflé and a pancake, which is like combining the best of two worlds. Either way, there's no reason to consider this breakfast a splurge, since there is no flour or added sugar. If you're really in the mood to treat yourself, top the cooked pancake with either melted butter, a drizzle of coconut milk or a very light dusting of icing sugar.

Preheat oven to 200°C/400°F/Gas Mark 6.

Heat butter in a 25-cm (10-in) ovenproof frying pan over a medium heat. Add the berries and simmer for 3–5 minutes so the liquid thickens.

While the berries simmer, use an electric mixer to beat the egg whites until stiff peaks form.

In a separate bowl, whisk the egg yolks for 1–2 minutes by hand with the vanilla and cinnamon. Gently fold the yolks into the egg whites.

With the heat under the fruit still at medium, spread the egg batter evenly on top of the fruit. Cook 2 minutes without touching, then transfer the pan to the oven. Bake for 10–12 minutes until the batter is puffed up slightly and lightly browned.

Remove the pan from the oven. Place a plate over the pan and flip the pan to invert the soufflé so the fruit is faced up. Eat warm or at room temperature.

Macronutrient Profile (per serving)

	Grams	Calories	%-Cals
Calories		176	
Fat	15	132	75%
Saturated	7	65	37%
Polyunsaturated	1	12	7%
Monounsaturated	5	42	24%
Carbohydrate	4	14	8%
Dietary Fibre	1		
Protein	7	27	15%

PRIMAL HOT CEREAL

Time in the Kitchen: 10 minutes
Servings: 2

- 75 g (2¾ oz) almonds, whole or flaked
- 75 g (2¾ oz) pecans
- ½ banana
- ¼ teaspoon ground cinnamon
- ⅛ teaspoon salt
- 60 ml (2 fl oz) unsweetened almond milk or coconut milk, plus more to taste

Some mornings, a bowl of creamy hot cereal sounds just right. This version contains no grains but tastes even better than an old fashioned bowl of porridge. I like the combination of almonds and pecans, but you can experiment with your favourite nuts. All the protein and healthy fats in this cereal will fill you up fast.

Pulse all ingredients in a food processor or blender until desired consistency is reached. Depending on your preference, the hot cereal can be smooth and creamy or chunky.

Warm the cereal in the microwave or on the hob until hot. Add fresh berries and more almond or coconut milk to taste.

Macronutrient Profile (per serving)

	Grams	Calories	%-Cals
Calories		487	
Fat	45	373	77%
Saturated	9	79	16%
Polyunsaturated	10	86	18%
Monounsaturated	23	190	39%
Carbohydrate	19	75	15%
Dietary Fibre	8		
Protein	11	38	8%

CREAMY COCONUT SQUASH

Time in the Kitchen: 20 minutes
Servings: 3–4 *(macronutrient profile based on 4 servings)*

½ butternut squash

350 ml (12 fl oz) coconut milk

¼ teaspoon cinnamon

40 g (1½ oz) pecans or other nuts

A smooth and creamy purée of butternut squash is a nice change of pace from bacon and eggs. The natural sweetness of the squash is complemented by the sweetness of the coconut milk and the warm flavour of cinnamon, making this a breakfast that is comforting to kids and adults alike.

Scoop the seeds and pulp out of the squash and peel the outside with a vegetable peeler. Cut the squash into small chunks and microwave until soft, about six minutes.

Place the squash in the food processor and blend until smooth. While blade is still running, add coconut milk and cinnamon.

Serve warm in a bowl, garnished with nuts and a generous knob of butter or an extra drizzle of coconut milk.

Macronutrient Profile (per serving)

	Grams	Calories	%-Cals
Calories		292	
Fat	27	223	77%
Saturated	20	163	56%
Polyunsaturated	2	16	5%
Monounsaturated	4	31	11%
Carbohydrate	15	57	19%
Dietary Fibre	6		
Protein	4	12	4%

CAULIFLOWER PURÉE WITH SAUSAGE AND POACHED EGGS

Time in the Kitchen: 15 minutes
Servings: 1–2 *(macronutrient profile based on 2 servings)*

225 g (8 oz) sausage, sliced into chunks

½ head cauliflower, broken into florets

1–2 tablespoons butter, or more to taste

salt to taste

1–2 eggs

1 tablespoon finely chopped parsley

This dish was inspired by an American traditional bowl of creamy Southern grits. The mild flavour and creamy texture of puréed cauliflower is a healthy Primal stand-in. Adding soft poached eggs and sausage creates a dish that instantly turns into comfort food.

If you eat dairy, adding a little cream or grated cheese to the cauliflower purée will create a richer, even creamier texture.

Set a small pot of water on to boil for the poached eggs.

Sauté the sausage in a pan over a medium heat until cooked through.

While the sausage is cooking, microwave (or steam) the cauliflower until soft, then purée in blender or food processor with the butter. Add salt to taste.

When the water comes to a very gentle boil, crack an egg in a bowl or cup then slide it carefully into the water. Let the egg cook for several minutes, until the egg white is hard and the yolk is cloudy. Scoop the poached egg out of the water with a slotted spoon.

Mix the sausage in with the cauliflower purée. Top with a poached egg and garnish with parsley.

Macronutrient Profile (per serving)

	Grams	Calories	%-Cals
Calories		**573**	
Fat	**49**	**439**	**77%**
Saturated	19	172	30%
Polyunsaturated	6	49	9%
Monounsaturated	19	170	30%
Carbohydrate	**3**	**12**	**2%**
Dietary Fibre	2		
Protein	**30**	**123**	**21%**

Quick & Easy Tip:

What to do with the other half of the cauliflower? Use it to make **Vegetable Coconut Stew** (page 114) or the **Korean Cauliflower Rice Bowl** (page 128).

TURKISH EGGS

Time in the Kitchen: 15 minutes
Servings: 1 (can easily be multiplied)

60 g (2¼ oz) plain full-fat yogurt

1 large garlic clove, finely chopped

1 tablespoon white wine vinegar or apple cider vinegar

1 egg

2 tablespoons unsalted butter

1 tablespoon finely chopped parsley

¼ teaspoon paprika

a pinch of chilli flakes or cayenne

a pinch of salt

If you've grown bored of omelettes and scrambles, this heavenly dish will make you feel like you're eating eggs again for the first time. A poached egg drizzled in paprika and parsley-spiked butter and set on a cushion of full-fat yogurt and garlic is a revelation.

If you can find sweet Hungarian paprika, it will have much more flavour than regular paprika sold in most supermarkets.

Stir yogurt and garlic together and spread on a plate. Set aside.

Fill a frying pan or small pot with 5–7.5 cm (2–3 in) of water. Add vinegar and bring to a very light simmer. Carefully crack the egg into a small cup. Very gently, slide the egg into the simmering water. Cook the egg undisturbed for 2–4 minutes, until the egg white is cooked. If the egg has stuck slightly to the bottom, first use a plastic spatula to loosen it, then lift the egg out of the water with a slotted spoon. Place the egg on top of the yogurt.

Over a medium heat, melt the butter and add parsley, paprika, chilli flakes and salt. Turn off the heat when the butter begins to sizzle and brown. Drizzle the butter on top of the egg.

Macronutrient Profile (per serving)

	Grams	Calories	%-Cals
Calories		322	
Fat	30	266	83%
Saturated	17	154	48%
Polyunsaturated	2	15	5%
Monounsaturated	8	75	23%
Carbohydrate	5	18	6%
Dietary Fibre	0		
Protein	9	36	11%

BUTTERY EGGS AND LEEKS

Time in the Kitchen: 20 minutes
Servings: 2

4 leeks

3 tablespoons butter

3 tablespoons double cream (optional)

6 eggs

2–4 rashers cooked bacon, crumbled

Even without the cream, you'll find this combination of silky scrambled eggs and leeks to be a luxuriously satisfying meal. As leeks cook, they become buttery and sweet in their own right and the mild flavour is a perfect pairing with eggs. Add some crumbled bacon on top and this simple dish is downright divine.

Trim the darker green tops off the leeks and slice the lighter green/white bottom section in half lengthways. Rinse each leek well, then slice crossways into thin strips.

Melt 2 tablespoons of butter in a frying pan over a medium-low heat and add the leeks, sautéing gently for a few minutes before putting a lid on the pan and letting the leeks cook for 8–10 minutes until very soft. Keep the heat low and stir occasionally; a little browning is okay, but mostly you just want the leeks to get soft.

While the leeks are cooking, whisk the eggs with 1 tablespoon of cream and a pinch of salt and pepper. Warm the remaining tablespoon of butter in a pan over a low heat then add the eggs. Keep the heat low and stir the eggs constantly as they cook so they don't brown and become too firm. When the eggs are cooked but still a bit loose and soft, remove from heat and divide on two plates.

Stir remaining 2 tablespoons of cream into the leeks and season with salt if needed. Spoon leeks over scrambled eggs and garnish with crumbled bacon.

Macronutrient Profile (per serving)

	Grams	Calories	%-Cals
Calories		477	
Fat	40	356	75%
Saturated	18	158	33%
Polyunsaturated	4	37	8%
Monounsaturated	14	122	26%
Carbohydrate	7	25	5%
Dietary Fibre	1		
Protein	23	96	20%

Quick & Easy Tip:

For convenience, cook a whole package of bacon at once, then freeze small portions to use as needed. Wrap the individual portions in paper towels then place in a sealed plastic bag. The frozen bacon will keep 4–6 weeks in the freezer and can go directly into a frying pan or be re-heated in a microwave.

FENNEL AND OLIVE OMELETTE

Time in the Kitchen: 20 minutes
Servings: 2 omelettes

4 tablespoons olive oil

1 fennel bulb, thinly sliced (fronds removed)

2–3 garlic cloves

2 tomatoes, chopped

15 g (½ oz) finely chopped fresh basil

90 g (3¼ oz) stoned olives

salt to taste

6 eggs, beaten

feta or goat's cheese (optional)

If you're tired of throwing the most obvious foods into your morning omelette – mushrooms, spinach, sausage – then this Mediterranean-flavoured omelette is just for you. While it's delicious for breakfast, don't hesitate to make this omelette for dinner, too.

Warm 2 tablespoons of olive oil in a frying pan over a medium-high heat and add fennel, sautéing until lightly browned. Add garlic and tomatoes and sauté five minutes more. Transfer to a bowl and mix in olives and basil. Salt to taste.

Warm remaining olive oil in a skillet. Add half of the beaten eggs to the pan. As the eggs cook, use a spatula to lift the edges of the omelette and tilt the pan so uncooked egg comes in direct contact with the pan.

After about three minutes, when the eggs are mostly set, add half of tomato mixture to one side of the eggs. Using a spatula, fold the uncovered half of the omelette over the top; cook a minute more and slide onto plate.

Repeat to make second omelette.

Macronutrient Profile (per serving)

	Grams	Calories	%-Cals
Calories		578	
Fat	50	440	76%
Saturated	10	87	15%
Polyunsaturated	6	57	10%
Monounsaturated	30	264	46%
Carbohydrate	15	53	9%
Dietary Fibre	5		
Protein	21	86	15%

BROCCOLI QUICHE

Time in the Kitchen: 30 minutes
Servings: 4–6 *(macronutrient profile based on 6 servings)*

340 g (12 oz) broccoli florets

6 eggs

350 ml (12 fl oz) coconut milk
  or whole cream

1 tablespoon melted butter

¼ teaspoon nutmeg

¼ teaspoon pepper

¼ teaspoon salt

30–60 g (1¼–2¼ oz) cheese,
  grated (optional)

A crust-less quiche is just as rich and satisfying, and quicker to make, than quiche with a crust. You can use this basic recipe as a starting point, and add other ingredients to the quiche as well, such as cooked sausage and other vegetables.

Preheat oven to 220°C/425°F/Gas Mark 7.

Butter a 25-cm (10-in) round or 33x23-cm (13x9-in) square baking dish.

Cook broccoli in the microwave or in boiling water for 4 minutes.

Whisk together eggs, coconut milk/cream, butter, nutmeg, salt and pepper. Stir in broccoli (and cheese, if using).

Pour into baking dish with broccoli and bake 20 minutes until set in the middle.

Macronutrient Profile (per serving)

	Grams	Calories	%-Cals
Calories		282	
Fat	23	196	70%
Saturated	16	134	48%
Polyunsaturated	1	13	4%
Monounsaturated	4	32	11%
Carbohydrate	13	48	17%
Dietary Fibre	5		
Protein	10	38	13%

PIZZA FRITTATA

Time in the Kitchen: 15 minutes
Servings: 4–6 *(macronutrient profile based on 6 servings)*

2 Italian sausages, sliced, or 225 g (8 oz) minced meat

120 g (4 oz) mushrooms, sliced

1 tomato, chopped

6 beaten eggs

15 g (½ oz) fresh basil, finely chopped

1 teaspoon dried oregano

30–60 g (1¼–2¼ oz) mozzarella, grated (optional)

While this frittata is not exactly like pizza, it does have all the Italian flavour of a pizza pie without all the carbs. And it's even good cold – just wrap some up and pack it for lunch.

Preheat the grill to high.

Heat a little oil over a high heat in an ovenproof 25-cm (10-in) skillet then add sausage and mushrooms. Sauté until sausage is cooked through and mushrooms are soft and their moisture has evaporated.

Turn heat down to medium. Add tomatoes and sauté a few seconds then pour in eggs and sprinkle with basil and oregano.

Stir quickly, then let cook undisturbed until the eggs begin to set. Sprinkle cheese on top and put the frittata under the grill until the top is golden and the eggs are firm, 3–5 minutes.

Macronutrient Profile (per serving)

	Grams	Calories	%-Cals
Calories		144	
Fat	9	84	58%
Saturated	3	26	18%
Polyunsaturated	1	13	9%
Monounsaturated	4	34	23%
Carbohydrate	4	14	10%
Dietary Fibre	1		
Protein	12	47	32%

SPAGHETTI SQUASH OMELETTE

Time in the Kitchen: 15 minutes
Servings: 2

½ spaghetti squash

4 eggs

knob of butter or a few tablespoons olive oil

salt and pepper to taste

I'm not saying you should try to sneak healthy ingredients into dishes you feed your family without telling them, but if you wanted to try, this would be a great recipe to start with. The spaghetti squash added to the omelette makes the texture fluffier and moister than an all-egg omelette, but other than adding a little sweetness, has surprisingly little affect on the flavour. You can eat this omelette with a little butter on top, or stuff it with any fillings you'd use for a regular omelette.

Once the spaghetti squash is cut in half, scoop out the seeds and stringy pulp. Microwave 8 minutes. Use a fork to loosen the squash from the skin and scrape the strands of squash into a bowl.

Whisk the eggs, then mix them together with the spaghetti squash. If you like, add a little salt and pepper.

In a 25-cm (10-in) pan over a medium heat, warm butter or olive oil. The omelette will brown easily, so make sure to keep the heat on medium. Add half of the whisked eggs to the pan and quickly spread it out evenly. Leave to cook for one minute, only disturbing the omelette to lift the edges gently with a spatula and give the pan a shake to make sure the egg isn't sticking.

If you're adding fillings, add them now to the middle of the omelette. Put a lid on the pan and cook 1–2 minutes more.

Use a spatula to gently fold the omelette in half. Slide out of the pan. Pour remaining eggs in the frying pan and repeat the steps to make the second omelette.

Macronutrient Profile (per serving)

	Grams	Calories	%-Cals
Calories		227	
Fat	15	131	58%
Saturated	5	45	20%
Polyunsaturated	2	20	9%
Monounsaturated	5	49	22%
Carbohydrate	11	41	18%
Dietary Fibre	2		
Protein	13	55	24%

PORTOBELLO MUSHROOMS STUFFED WITH EGGS AND SPINACH

Time in the Kitchen: 25 minutes
Servings: 4

4 large portobello mushrooms, stems removed

125 ml (4 fl oz) olive oil

300 g (11 oz) frozen or fresh spinach

6 eggs, whisked

125–225 g (4–8 oz) minced meat, sausage or crumbled bacon (optional)

Portobello mushrooms act as an edible bowl in this recipe, contributing both extra flavour and visual appeal to simple scrambled eggs. This is an impressive dish to serve for brunch.

Preheat oven to 220°C/425°F/Gas Mark 7.

Drizzle olive oil over both sides of portobello mushrooms. Lightly salt and pepper mushrooms. Place mushrooms on a baking sheet in the oven for 15 minutes.

While mushrooms are baking, sauté spinach with a little bit of oil. Add meat or bacon (if using) and sauté until meat is cooked, then turn heat to low and add eggs. Stir eggs, cooking until they reach your desired consistency.

Remove mushrooms from the oven and fill with scrambled eggs.

Macronutrient Profile (per serving)

	Grams	Calories	%-Cals
Calories		401	
Fat	37	326	81%
Saturated	7	58	15%
Polyunsaturated	5	41	10%
Monounsaturated	23	207	52%
Carbohydrate	7	25	6%
Dietary Fibre	4		
Protein	14	50	12%

BREAKFAST BURRITO

Time in the Kitchen: 25 minutes
Servings: 2 burritos

4 eggs, whites and yolks separated

½ onion, finely chopped

1–2 tomatoes, finely chopped

60 g (2¼ oz) canned diced green chillies

1 red pepper cut into strips

15 g (½ oz) coriander, finely chopped

175 g (6 oz) cooked meat (try sliced steak, minced beef or shredded chicken)

1 avocado, cut into wedges or small chunks

hot sauce or salsa on the side (optional)

More interesting than a regular scramble and a bit different from an omelette, this breakfast burrito can hold almost any combination of ingredients. I'm a fan of this south of the border version that makes use of whatever meat you have leftover from dinner the night before.

Whisk the egg whites.

Warm a lightly oiled 25-cm (10-in) frying pan. Pour half the egg whites in the pan, swirling the pan around so the whites spread thinly and evenly. After about 30 seconds, put a lid on the pan and cook 1 minute more. Use a rubber spatula to loosen and slide the egg white 'tortilla' onto a plate. Repeat once more with the remaining egg whites.

In the same pan, sauté onions with oil for one minute then add tomato, green chillies, red pepper, coriander and meat.

Whisk egg yolks and pour into the pan, mixing into a scramble with the other ingredients.

Add avocado at the very end, then spoon half of filling onto each egg white. Roll the egg whites up into burritos and serve with hot sauce or salsa.

Macronutrient Profile (per serving)

	Grams	Calories	%-Cals
Calories		524	
Fat	35	308	59%
Saturated	8	74	14%
Polyunsaturated	5	44	8%
Monounsaturated	18	157	30%
Carbohydrate	30	111	21%
Dietary Fibre	11		
Protein	27	106	20%

BEEF BREAKFAST PATTIES

Time in the Kitchen: 25 minutes
Servings: 12 small patties *(macronutrient profile based on serving size of 3 patties)*

450 g (1 lb) lean beef mince
¼ onion, finely chopped
¼–½ teaspoon salt
½ teaspoon black pepper or cayenne
¼ teaspoon cinnamon
¼ teaspoon allspice
1 tablespoon finely chopped rosemary
1 tablespoon finely chopped parsley

Lean beef mince is a good choice for quick cooking because it's best slightly pink. The lower fat content means well-done lean beef will be dry, so I pan-fry these succulent breakfast patties for only 6–8 minutes. The spices and herbs in this recipe give the patties a slightly sweet flavour that's similar to shop-bought breakfast sausage, only better.

Fry up a batch of these early in the week and then grab a few out of the fridge each morning for breakfast (or an afternoon snack).

Mix together all ingredients in a bowl.

With your hands, form meat into 12 rounded patties, about 1 cm (½ in) thick.

Warm a little oil in a pan over a medium-high heat and cook patties about 3 minutes on the first side and slightly longer on the second side, until nicely browned and slightly pink in the middle.

Macronutrient Profile (per serving)

	Grams	Calories	%-Cals
Calories		277	
Fat	17	157	57%
Saturated	7	67	24%
Polyunsaturated	1	8	3%
Monounsaturated	7	61	22%
Carbohydrate	1	5	2%
Dietary Fibre	0		
Protein	27	116	42%

ESPRESSO RUBBED STEAK

Time in the Kitchen: 15 minutes
Servings: 2–4 *(macronutrient profile based on 4 servings)*

2 teaspoons chilli powder

2 tablespoons finely ground espresso

½ teaspoon kosher salt

¼ teaspoon ground black pepper

450 g (1 lb) flank or skirt steak

This recipe is for all you coffee lovers who can't resist the aroma of espresso brewing in the morning. A rub flavoured with ground espresso gives steak a deep, rich and pleasantly bitter flavour – just like a cup o' joe. Although instant espresso will work, grinding fresh beans is preferred.

Mix together the chilli powder, ground espresso, salt and black pepper. Rub the mixture into the steak, covering it completely. Slice the steak into thin strips.

Heat a little bit of oil in a pan over a high heat and add the steak, searing for 4–6 minutes or until it reaches desired doneness.

Macronutrient Profile (per serving)

	Grams	Calories	%-Cals
Calories		218	
Fat	10	86	39%
Saturated	4	35	16%
Polyunsaturated	0	4	2%
Monounsaturated	4	34	15%
Carbohydrate	1	2	1%
Dietary Fibre	0		
Protein	32	135	60%

SMOKED SALMON, EGG AND ASPARAGUS ROLL UPS

Time in the Kitchen: 20 minutes
Servings: 12 roll ups *(macronutrient profile based on serving size of 3 roll ups)*

12 asparagus spears

12 eggs

½ red onion, thinly sliced

225 g (8 oz) wild smoked salmon

You could throw all these ingredients into an omelette, but why, when these roll ups are so much more fun to eat? Kids especially love this healthy finger food for breakfast and adults love Smoked Salmon, Egg and Asparagus Roll Ups as a starter.

Slice or snap off the bottom 5–10 cm (2–4 in) of the asparagus spears. In boiling water or in the microwave, cook asparagus 3–5 minutes until it softens but is still fairly firm.

Whisk the eggs. Warm a 25-cm (10-in) or smaller frying pan with a little oil or butter in it and pour 2–3 tablespoons of egg in, swirling the pan around to evenly spread the egg into a very thin layer. Let the egg cook about 1 minute until firm, then slide out of the pan. Repeat until eggs are gone.

Lay an egg 'crêpe' on a flat surface. On one end of the crêpe, layer salmon with an asparagus spear and slices of onion. Roll the crêpe up. Repeat with remaining crêpes and asparagus spears.

Macronutrient Profile (per serving)

	Grams	Calories	%-Cals
Calories		334	
Fat	21	188	56%
Saturated	6	54	16%
Polyunsaturated	4	32	10%
Monounsaturated	8	76	23%
Carbohydrate	5	20	6%
Dietary Fibre	1		
Protein	30	127	38%

STEAK WITH ROMESCO SAUCE

Time in the Kitchen: 15 minutes
Servings: 2

225 g (8 oz) skirt steak, or other cut of steak

150 g (5 oz) cherry tomatoes

40 g (1½ oz) almonds, whole or sliced

2 garlic cloves

1 roasted red pepper

60 ml (2 fl oz) olive oil

1 tablespoon sherry vinegar

¼ teaspoon chilli flakes

Romesco is a Spanish sauce made from tomatoes, red peppers, garlic and almonds. Nutritious and flavourful, it can be served with any type of meat or seafood. It also tastes great with eggs, so don't hesitate to scramble a few up to serve alongside the steak.

Roasted red peppers are sold in supermarkets and save time, but you can also roast your own. Simply blacken the red pepper under a grill or over an open flame, let the pepper cool, then remove the burnt skin under running water.

Skirt steak is usually thin enough that it will cook quickly, so you don't necessarily need to slice it before cooking. If you're using a thicker cut of steak, however, speed up the cooking time by slicing it thinly and then cooking it.

Heat a frying pan over a medium-high heat. Lightly salt and pepper the steak. Place it on one side of the pan and the tomatoes, almonds and garlic cloves on the other side.

Stir the tomatoes, almonds and garlic a few times, so they brown evenly. After 3 minutes, flip the steak. Cook 2 minutes more and scoop the tomatoes, garlic and almonds into a food processor or blender. Keep the steak in the pan and continue to cook until done (thinly sliced steak will only need a few minutes more).

Add the roasted red pepper, olive oil, sherry vinegar and chilli flakes to the food processor or blender and pulse until smooth.

Serve the Romesco sauce drizzled over the steak.

Macronutrient Profile (per serving)

	Grams	Calories	%-Cals
Calories		632	
Fat	50	440	70%
Saturated	10	87	14%
Polyunsaturated	6	49	8%
Monounsaturated	32	284	45%
Carbohydrate	13	48	8%
Dietary Fibre	4		
Protein	35	144	23%

BACON AND EGG SALAD

Time in the Kitchen: 15 minutes
Servings: 2–4 *(macronutrient profile based on 4 servings)*

1 small head frisée

1 small head Romaine or cos

150–225 g (5–8 oz) bacon or pancetta, cut into small pieces

1 shallot, finely chopped

3 tablespoons sherry vinegar

1 tablespoon mustard

2–4 eggs

The flavour elements in this traditional French salad, often called Salad Lyonnaise, come together in this perfect breakfast salad. Frisée is the traditional lettuce used, but if you find it to be too 'weedy', substitute fresh spinach or rocket.

Tear the heads of frisée and romaine into bite-sized pieces and toss in a bowl.

Sauté the bacon until crisp. Keeping the heat on medium, add the shallot. Sauté a few minutes then add vinegar and mustard. Stir as it boils for about 20 seconds then remove from the heat and pour over the lettuce.

The salad can be served with either poached or fried eggs. To fry, simply heat oil or butter in a pan and cook eggs until they reach desired doneness. To poach, bring a small pot of water to a gentle boil. Crack an egg in a bowl or cup, then slide it carefully into the water. Let the egg cook for several minutes until the egg white is hard and the yolk is cloudy.

Macronutrient Profile (per serving)

	Grams	Calories	%-Cals
Calories		422	
Fat	29	265	63%
Saturated	9	85	20%
Polyunsaturated	4	32	8%
Monounsaturated	13	113	27%
Carbohydrate	9	34	8%
Dietary Fibre	4		
Protein	30	122	29%

TURNIP HASH BROWNS

Time in the Kitchen: 25 minutes
Servings: 2

1 large turnip, or 2 small,
   peeled and grated
2–4 spring onions, thinly sliced
3 tablespoons butter

Turnips have a texture much like potatoes and a very mild, slightly sweet flavour. They don't get quite get as brown and crispy as potato hash browns do, but they're just as delicious.

For protein, scramble an egg in with the hash browns. For variation, try making these hash browns with mooli or daikon and a drizzle of tamari.

Wrap grated turnip in a thin tea towel and wring out as much excess liquid as possible.

In a frying pan over a medium heat, melt butter then add the turnip and spring onions, mixing well to coat the turnip with butter. Cook 10–15 minutes until turnip is nicely browned, stirring only occasionally.

Macronutrient Profile (per serving)

	Grams	Calories	%-Cals
Calories		196	
Fat	17	154	78%
Saturated	11	97	49%
Polyunsaturated	1	7	3%
Monounsaturated	5	40	20%
Carbohydrate	10	38	19%
Dietary Fibre	4		
Protein	2	5	3%

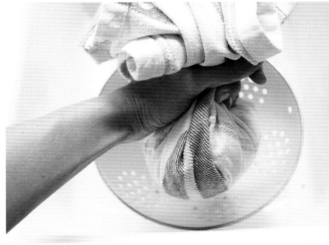

BACON SOUFFLÉ FRITTATA

Time in the Kitchen: 25 minutes
Servings: 4

2 tablespoons butter

6 eggs, separated into whites and yolks

8–10 rashers bacon

This breakfast dish manages to be light, fluffy, rich, and filling all at the same time. It's good hot or cold, so don't hesitate to make the soufflé frittata at night so the next morning you can eat a slice as a quick breakfast-to-go.

Preheat oven to 180°C/350°F/Gas Mark 4.

Melt two tablespoons of butter and set it aside to cool.

In a 30-cm (12-in) frying pan, fry the bacon until it reaches desired doneness. Remove bacon from pan (leave remaining fat in the pan) and crumble the bacon into pieces.

While the bacon is frying, use an electric mixer to beat the egg whites until stiff peaks form.

In a separate bowl, whisk together the egg yolks and melted butter by hand.

Gently fold egg yolks and bacon pieces into the egg whites.

Warm the frying pan with bacon fat over a medium heat and pour the batter in evenly. Leave to cook untouched for two minutes, then move the pan into the oven and bake for 15 minutes.

Remove from oven and loosen from pan with a rubber spatula.

	Grams	Calories	%-Cals
Calories		284	
Fat	23	209	73%
Saturated	9	81	29%
Polyunsaturated	3	23	8%
Monounsaturated	9	79	28%
Carbohydrate	1	5	2%
Dietary Fibre	0		
Protein	17	71	25%

PORK AND RADISH HASH

Time in the Kitchen: 20 minutes
Servings: 2

2   tablespoons butter, bacon
    fat or olive oil

½   white or yellow onion, finely
    chopped

1   large bunch of radishes
    (about 10 radishes), chopped
    into small pieces

450–675 g (1–1½ lb) cooked
    pork, cut into small pieces

125 ml (4 fl oz) or chicken stock

15 g (½ oz) parsley, finely
    chopped

    salt and pepper to taste

If you have some leftover pork in the fridge, then this is the breakfast dish for you (hint: it's especially good with pork that's been seasoned with the *Fennel and Lemon Rub* (page 216). Don't waste time making sure the radishes and pork are perfectly diced – hash is not about perfection; it's meant to be a deliciously messy dish.

Melt the fat in a frying pan over a medium heat and add onion and radishes. Sauté five minutes.

Add pork and stock. Simmer five more minutes until liquid is evaporated. Garnish with parsley.

Add salt and pepper to taste.

	Grams	Calories	%-Cals
Calories		547	
Fat	31	279	51%
Saturated	14	129	24%
Polyunsaturated	2	19	3%
Monounsaturated	12	106	19%
Carbohydrate	4	15	3%
Dietary Fibre	1		
Protein	59	252	46%

SAVOURY SMOOTHIE

Time in the Kitchen: 5 minutes
Servings: 1

1 tomato
1 handful of lettuce or greens
(try watercress, spinach
or kale)
½ avocado
1 teaspoon hot sauce or more
to taste
a few ice cubes

This smoothie is like a salad in a glass. For those mornings when you don't have time to sit down and eat, blend everything together and away you go!

Mix everything in a blender until smooth.

Macronutrient Profile (per serving)

Calories		190	
Fat	15	126	67%
Saturated	2	18	10%
Polyunsaturated	2	17	9%
Monounsaturated	10	83	44%
Carbohydrate	15	52	27%
Dietary Fibre	9		
Protein	4	11	6%

Quick & Easy Tip:

Saving half an avocado for later? To keep the beautiful green colour from turning an unappetizing brown, take out the stone and rub olive oil on the surface, then pour a little oil in a bowl. Set the avocado face down in the bowl and refrigerate.

ROCKET AND BLUEBERRY SALAD WITH RASPBERRY VINAIGRETTE

Time in the Kitchen: 15 minutes
Servings: 2

150 g (5 oz) blueberries

4 handfuls of rocket

100 g (3½ oz) walnuts

1–2 avocados, cut into chunks

60 ml (2 fl oz) walnut oil

1 tablespoon white wine vinegar

1 tablespoon honey

30 g (1¼ oz) raspberries

salt to taste

Yes, this salad is bursting with healthy antioxidants and omega oils, but it's also bursting with flavour. Peppery rocket, sweet, tart berries, creamy avocado and savoury walnuts are a magical combination. The raspberry vinaigrette is amazing when made with walnut oil, but olive oil can be substituted if desired.

In a large bowl, mix together blueberries, rocket, walnuts and avocado.

In a blender, combine walnut oil, vinegar, honey and raspberries until well-blended and smooth. Add salt to taste.

Drizzle raspberry dressing over salad, toss and serve.

Macronutrient Profile (per serving)

	Grams	Calories	%-Cals
Calories		967	
Fat	89	759	78%
Saturated	9	80	8%
Polyunsaturated	49	415	43%
Monounsaturated	26	224	23%
Carbohydrate	44	162	17%
Dietary Fibre	18		
Protein	14	47	5%

The Primal Blueprint Quick & Easy Cookbook

WATER CHESTNUT FRUIT SALAD

Time in the Kitchen: 15 minutes
Servings: 3–4 *(macronutrient profile based on 4 servings)*

1 can water chestnuts, drained, or 1 jicama, peeled and cut into cubes

1 cucumber, sliced

125 g (4 oz) raspberries

165 g (5¾ oz) pineapple chunks (optional)

juice of 1 lemon or lime

1 teaspoon chilli powder (less spicy) or cayenne pepper (more spicy)

a pinch of salt

In Los Angeles, outdoor stands selling freshly cut fruit salad with chilli powder and lime are easy to find. My Mexican fruit salad takes its inspiration from this refreshing and healthy snack, but I throw in some raspberries for an added boost of antioxidants. The lemon or lime, chilli and just a pinch of salt really make the flavours pop.

Simply combine all ingredients in a large bowl and serve. This salad tastes best when it's cold, so consider refrigerating the ingredients beforehand.

Macronutrient Profile (per serving)

	Grams	Calories	%-Cals
Calories		90	
Fat	**1**	**5**	**5%**
Saturated	0	1	1%
Polyunsaturated	0	2	2%
Monounsaturated	0	1	0%
Carbohydrate	**21**	**80**	**88%**
Dietary Fibre	11		
Protein	**2**	**6**	**7%**

ORANGE OLIVE CHICKEN

Time in the Kitchen: 20 minutes
Servings: 4

2 teaspoons paprika

2 garlic cloves, crushed

4 tablespoons olive oil

2 tablespoons sherry vinegar

450–675 g (1–1½ lb) chicken breast, cut into 2.5-cm (1-in) cubes

1 orange

15 g (½ oz) parsley, finely chopped

90 g (3¼ oz) stoned black olives (try Moroccan oil-cured or Greek Kalamata)

¼ teaspoon chilli flakes

If oranges and olives sound like a strange combination, know that Moroccan cuisine has celebrated the pairing for centuries. When you try this salad, you'll know why – it's a case of wildly different flavours coming together in perfect harmony.

The idea for this salad was inspired by a Spicy Orange Salad recipe published by the New York Times. I add chicken for a protein boost that turns the salad into a full meal. You really only need one orange to add the necessary citrus flavour to this salad, so make sure to choose one that's as flavourful as possible. Valencia oranges are especially juicy in summer months, and Cara Cara are a good choice in winter and spring.

Whisk together paprika, garlic, olive oil and vinegar.

Lightly salt the chicken. Pour half of the vinaigrette over the chicken. Cook the chicken under a grill on high for 10–12 minutes until done.

While the chicken is cooking, peel the orange, trimming away as much white pulp as possible. Cut each orange wedge in half or into thirds.

In a serving bowl, combine the orange pieces, parsley, olives and chilli flakes. Add the cooked chicken and drizzle remaining vinaigrette on top. Toss gently to blend. Serve cold or at room temperature.

Macronutrient Profile (per serving)

	Grams	Calories	%-Cals
Calories		440	
Fat	22	191	44%
Saturated	4	34	8%
Polyunsaturated	3	27	6%
Monounsaturated	13	118	27%
Carbohydrate	6	21	5%
Dietary Fibre	2		
Protein	53	226	52%

TROPICAL AVOCADO AND PRAWNS

Time in the Kitchen: 25 minutes
Servings: 4

½ ripe mango, peeled and cut into chunks

1 jalapeño or green chilli, seeds and membrane removed

60 ml (2 fl oz) fresh lime juice (about 2 limes)

60 ml (2 fl oz) plus 1 tablespoon olive oil

¼ teaspoon salt

450 g (1 lb) uncooked prawns, peeled and deveined

1 teaspoon cumin

2 avocados, cut into small chunks

6 radishes, thinly sliced

½ red onion, thinly sliced

15 g (½ oz) coriander, finely chopped

This light and refreshing salad will whisk your taste buds away to a tropical island. Mango and prawns pair especially well together, and the radish and jalapeño contribute just enough spiciness to balance out the sweetness of the fruit.

In a food processor or blender, purée mango, jalapeño, lime juice, olive oil and salt. Set aside in the refrigerator.

Sprinkle the prawns with cumin, then sauté or grill for about 5 minutes until cooked.

In a large bowl, combine prawns, avocado, radish, red onion and coriander. Toss with dressing and serving chilled or at room temperature.

Macronutrient Profile (per serving)

	Grams	Calories	%-Cals
Calories		376	
Fat	21	178	47%
Saturated	3	27	7%
Polyunsaturated	3	28	7%
Monounsaturated	13	109	29%
Carbohydrate	18	63	17%
Dietary Fibre	8		
Protein	32	135	36%

CRANBERRY TUNA SALAD

Time in the Kitchen: 10 minutes
Servings: 2

350 g (12 oz) canned tuna

2   celery sticks, finely chopped

40 g (1½ oz) red onion, finely chopped

60 ml (2 fl oz) mayonnaise, or more to taste

60 g (2¼ oz) dried cranberries

This unusually delicious combination of tuna and tart, sweet dried cranberries takes plain old tuna salad to a new level. It's an easy lunch to pack up for work – simply eat it with a spoon or toss the tuna with mixed lettuce. Potentially elevated mercury levels have turned canned tuna into an occasional meal, not something I'd eat every week. However, it's a convenient protein-rich meal that can be enjoyed on occasion.

Simply mix ingredients together in a bowl.

Macronutrient Profile (per serving)

	Grams	Calories	%-Cals
Calories		487	
Fat	23	207	42%
Saturated	4	33	7%
Polyunsaturated	13	111	23%
Monounsaturated	6	51	10%
Carbohydrate	27	98	20%
Dietary Fibre	3		
Protein	43	183	37%

SESAME WHITE FISH SALAD

Time in the Kitchen: 15 minutes
Servings: 2–4 *(macronutrient profile based on 4 servings)*

450 g (1 lb) cod, or other white fish

4 tablespoons sesame oil for the dressing, plus a few tablespoons more to cook the fish

4 tablespoons mayonnaise

1 tablespoon rice wine vinegar

1 tablespoon sesame seeds, lightly toasted in a pan

55 g (2 oz) spring onions or salad onions, chopped

Cod and other types of white fish, like halibut, are a tasty alternative when tuna salad gets boring. This particular recipe gives cod a bit of Asian flavour and is delicious served over lettuce or wrapped in lettuce leaves. Feel free to embellish this white fish salad with avocado – you won't be sorry.

To cook the fish, drizzle with a few tablespoons of sesame oil and sprinkle with salt. Grill on high for five minutes on each side.

Flake the fish into pieces, then put in the refrigerator to chill while you make the dressing.

Mix together 4 tablespoons of sesame oil, mayonnaise and vinegar. Drizzle over fish then add sesame seeds and spring onions. Stir well to coat fish.

Macronutrient Profile (per serving)

	Grams	Calories	%-Cals
Calories		423	
Fat	34	299	71%
Saturated	5	43	10%
Polyunsaturated	16	137	32%
Monounsaturated	12	102	24%
Carbohydrate	2	9	2%
Dietary Fibre	1		
Protein	27	115	27%

JALAPEÑO EGG SALAD

Time in the Kitchen: 25 minutes
Servings: 2

6 eggs

1 tablespoon finely chopped chives

1 jalapeño or green chilli, seeds removed, finely chopped

60 ml (2 fl oz) mayonnaise

1 tablespoon lemon juice, or more to taste

For Homemade Mayonnaise:

2 egg yolks

1 teaspoon mustard

1 tablespoon lemon juice, or more to taste

225 ml (8 fl oz) oil

salt to taste

Slightly spicy jalapeño chilli and bright, tart lemon juice add a lot of flavour to egg salad. Sliced into tiny pieces, the jalapeño's flavour is subtle. Sliced into larger rings, the pepper leaves more of an impression on the palate.

To make recipes like this easy to whip up, it helps to regularly make condiments like homemade mayonnaise so they're always on hand.

Place eggs in a small pot with enough cold water to cover the eggs completely. Bring to the boil over a high heat. As soon as the water begins to boil, turn off the heat and cover the pot. Leave to stand for 10 minutes, then transfer eggs to a bowl filled with ice cubes and water. Chill eggs for five minutes or so, then peel.

If you don't have any homemade mayonnaise on hand, make a batch while the eggs cook.

Chop the eggs into small pieces. Combine in a bowl with the remaining ingredients.

To make Homemade Mayonnaise:

Whisk together egg yolks, mustard and lemon juice. Add oil slowly, continually whisking as you drizzle it in. Whisk until the mayo has a thick consistency. Season with salt. Homemade mayonnaise will keep for several days in the refrigerator.

Macronutrient Profile (per serving)

	Grams	Calories	%-Cals
Calories		434	
Fat	37	335	77%
Saturated	8	73	17%
Polyunsaturated	14	123	29%
Monounsaturated	12	103	24%
Carbohydrate	4	14	3%
Dietary Fibre	0		
Protein	19	84	19%

KALE SALAD WITH AVOCADO AND HAZELNUTS

Time in the Kitchen: 15 minutes
Servings: 2–3 *(macronutrient profile based on 3 servings)*

juice from half an orange (about 60 ml (2 fl oz))

juice from half a lemon (about 2 tablespoons)

60 ml (2 fl oz) hazelnut oil

1 bunch kale

2 avocados, peeled and cut into chunks

75 g (2¾ oz) hazelnuts, roughly chopped

salt and pepper to taste

Incredibly healthy and incredibly tasty; that's what I call the perfect lunch. Dark, leafy greens like kale are considered one of the most nutrient-dense foods available, so fill up your salad bowl and add plenty of avocado and nuts for healthy fat and protein.

Hazelnut oil adds an extra-nutty flavour to this salad, but olive oil can be used as well.

Whisk together juices and oil in a bowl.

Remove the tough and chewy middle stem from each kale leaf by cutting it out with a knife, then thinly slice the kale leaves.

Toss kale with avocado and dressing and season to taste with salt and pepper. Sprinkle hazelnuts on top.

Macronutrient Profile (per serving)

	Grams	Calories	%-Cals
Calories		561	
Fat	50	428	76%
Saturated	5	44	8%
Polyunsaturated	6	52	9%
Monounsaturated	36	309	55%
Carbohydrate	29	105	19%
Dietary Fibre	13		
Protein	9	27	5%

Quick & Easy Tip:

Sometimes it's hard to get to the greens you've stored in the refrigerator before they wilt. Don't throw the greens out! Instead, revive them with a quick soak in ice water.

BROCCOLI WITH ALMOND DRESSING

Time in the Kitchen: 10 minutes
Servings: 2–4 *(macronutrient profile based on 4 servings)*

1 head of broccoli
1 tablespoon rice wine vinegar
2 tablespoons tahini
3 tablespoons almond butter
½ tablespoon honey
1 tablespoon sesame oil
2 tablespoons tamari
½ teaspoon chilli oil or chilli flakes (or more to taste)

This simple combination of broccoli smothered in an Asian almond dressing has enough richness and flavour to stand alone, but if you want to turn it into a complete meal, throw in some cooked steak or chicken. In fact, if you're out of broccoli, this dressing makes a great dip for beef or chicken skewers off the barbecue.

Cut the broccoli into florets. Microwave (about three minutes) or steam broccoli until it reaches desired tenderness.

Mix remaining ingredients together until they form a smooth dressing. Pour over broccoli and stir to cover. Serve warm or cold.

Macronutrient Profile (per serving)

	Grams	Calories	%-Cals
Calories		198	
Fat	15	127	64%
Saturated	2	15	8%
Polyunsaturated	5	41	21%
Monounsaturated	8	64	32%
Carbohydrate	14	51	26%
Dietary Fibre	4		
Protein	6	20	10%

Quick & Easy Tip:

Some of the ingredients for this recipe, like the tamari, almond butter and sesame oil, also come in handy when making *Chicken with Almond Coconut Dipping Sauce* (page 176).

CREAMY BASIL PESTO COLESLAW

Time in the Kitchen: 10 minutes
Servings: 2–4 *(macronutrient profile based on 4 servings)*

55 g (2 oz) walnuts (or pine nuts)

2 garlic cloves

60 ml (2 fl oz) coconut milk

200 g (7 oz) loosely packed basil leaves

60 ml (2 fl oz) olive oil

sea salt to taste

350 g (12 oz) cabbage, shredded (roughly half a head of cabbage)

60 ml (2 fl oz) rice wine vinegar

Coleslaw is generally served as a side dish, so plan on serving this with some sort of protein. I've served it with seafood, steak, chicken and pork and all have been winners. If you're not in the mood for coleslaw, then just make the pesto; it's good enough to eat with a spoon. The coconut milk adds the creaminess that cheese usually does, but doesn't add a strong coconut flavour.

Blend walnuts, garlic and coconut milk in a food processor until smooth. Add basil leaves and pulse several times to begin chopping up the leaves, then with the blade running, pour in olive oil. Continue to process until the basil leaves are blended in. Add salt to taste.

Combine pesto and cabbage, stirring well. Drizzle half of the rice wine vinegar over the cabbage and continue to mix; add remaining rice wine vinegar to taste.

Macronutrient Profile (per serving)

	Grams	Calories	%-Cals
Calories		335	
Fat	28	243	73%
Saturated	6	52	16%
Polyunsaturated	9	80	24%
Monounsaturated	12	101	31%
Carbohydrate	17	62	19%
Dietary Fibre	12		
Protein	9	26	8%

AUBERGINE AND FENNEL SALAD

Time in the Kitchen: 20 minutes
Servings: 2

1 large aubergine

1 fennel bulb, very thinly sliced (use a mandoline to slice if you have one)

60 ml (2 fl oz) olive oil

2 tablespoons sherry vinegar

1–2 garlic cloves, finely chopped

¼ teaspoon paprika

½ teaspoon salt

15 g (½ oz) parsley, finely chopped

1–2 spring onions or salad onions

Few people know that aubergine cooks incredibly well in the microwave. The texture is less oily and mushy than aubergine cooked on the hob and it only takes 6 minutes from start to finish. This salad has fantastic flavour and can be a meal in itself, although it pairs especially well with the ***Tahini Chicken Salad*** (page 74).

Cut the aubergine in half lengthways, then cut each half lengthways into quarters.

Place on a plate and cover (another plate works well for this) then microwave 6 minutes, until aubergine is soft and easy to pierce with a fork. Slice the aubergine into bite-sized pieces and combine in a bowl with fennel.

In a small bowl, whisk together olive oil, vinegar, garlic, paprika and salt. Pour over aubergine. Add parsley and spring onions to the bowl. Mix well.

Macronutrient Profile (per serving)

	Grams	Calories	%-Cals
Calories		386	
Fat	28	248	65%
Saturated	4	35	9%
Polyunsaturated	3	29	8%
Monounsaturated	20	176	46%
Carbohydrate	34	124	32%
Dietary Fibre	11		
Protein	4	12	3%

TAHINI CHICKEN SALAD

Time in the Kitchen: 20 minutes
Servings: 4

900 g (2 lb) chicken, cut into 2.5-cm (1-in) cubes

5 tablespoons olive oil

2 tablespoons tahini

2 tablespoons sherry vinegar

3 carrots, grated

6 radishes, sliced

25 g (1 oz) parsley, roughly chopped

sesame seeds to garnish

When you're tired of chicken salad with mayonnaise, this creamy dressing made from tahini is a welcome change. Tahini is simply a paste made from sesame seeds that is often used in Middle Eastern cooking. It can be found in most supermarkets and gives this salad a rich, nutty flavour.

Season the chicken lightly with salt and pepper and mix with 2 tablespoons of olive oil. Turn the grill to high and cook chicken for 10 minutes, stirring once or twice. Let cool slightly.

Whisk together the remaining olive oil, tahini and vinegar.

In a large bowl, mix chicken with carrots, radish and parsley. Drizzle dressing on top and mix well. Garnish with sesame seeds. Serve at room temperature or chilled.

Macronutrient Profile (per serving)

	Grams	Calories	%-Cals
Calories		645	
Fat	38	335	52%
Saturated	8	67	10%
Polyunsaturated	7	65	10%
Monounsaturated	20	176	27%
Carbohydrate	7	26	4%
Dietary Fibre	2		
Protein	67	284	44%

CHIMICHURRI STEAK SALAD

Time in the Kitchen: 20 minutes
Servings: 3

175 ml (6 fl oz) olive oil

60 ml (2 fl oz) sherry vinegar or red wine vinegar

2 garlic cloves, peeled

¼ teaspoon chilli flakes

1 tablespoon dried oregano leaves or 15 g (½ oz) fresh oregano leaves

1 large bunch fresh flat-leaf parsley, bottom part of stems cut off

450 g (1 lb) flank steak

3 large handfuls of lettuce

Chimichurri is an herb sauce that's especially popular in Argentina, a country known for serving amazing steak. Drizzled over steak and lettuce, the sauce becomes more of a dressing, which is only one of many uses you'll find for chimichurri. The piquant, lively flavours perk up everything from seafood to chicken and roasted vegetables.

Heat the barbecue to medium-high.

Combine the first five ingredients in a blender, then add parsley in small handfuls. Use a rubber spatula, spoon or butter knife to loosen and stir the leaves between blending them. Eventually, the sauce will be easier to blend; continue blending until it is smooth. Add a pinch of salt if needed.

Lightly salt and pepper the steak. Barbecue for six minutes on each side for medium-rare. Leave to stand 5 minutes before slicing steak and mixing it with lettuce. Serve chimichurri sauce drizzled over the salad.

Macronutrient Profile (per serving)

	Grams	Calories	%-Cals
Calories		794	
Fat	67	594	75%
Saturated	13	113	14%
Polyunsaturated	6	56	7%
Monounsaturated	45	395	50%
Carbohydrate	6	20	2%
Dietary Fibre	3		
Protein	44	183	23%

Quick & Easy Tip:

To quickly dry washed herbs, throw them into a salad spinner and give them a whirl.

The Primal Blueprint Quick & Easy Cookbook   **77**

ZESTY STEAK SALAD

Time in the Kitchen: 20 minutes
Servings: 4

- 1 head Romaine or cos lettuce, sliced thinly or broken into bite-sized leaves
- 1 small red onion, thinly sliced
- 2 jalapeños or green chillis, cut in half and deseeded, then thinly sliced
- 60 ml (2 fl oz) plus 1 tablespoon extra virgin olive oil
- 2 tablespoons Dijon mustard
- 1 tablespoon red wine vinegar
- 450 g (1 lb) flank steak, skirt steak, or sirloin steak
- salt and pepper to taste

This is a simple steak salad, but one you will love. Jalapeño chillies add just a hint of spice, and combined with the red onion gives the salad a zippy flavour and crunchy texture.

Combine lettuce, onion and pepper in a large bowl.

Whisk together 60 ml (2 fl oz) olive oil, 1 tablespoon mustard and the red wine vinegar. Drizzle over lettuce, onion and pepper.

Smear 1 tablespoon of mustard and 1 tablespoon of olive oil over both sides of the steak. Salt the steak lightly and sear in a pan over very high heat, or barbecue on high. It should only take a few minutes on each side. Remove from heat and slice thinly. Combine with lettuce. Add salt and pepper to taste.

Macronutrient Profile (per serving)

	Grams	Calories	%-Cals
Calories		404	
Fat	27	240	59%
Saturated	6	56	14%
Polyunsaturated	3	22	5%
Monounsaturated	16	145	35%
Carbohydrate	8	28	7%
Dietary Fibre	4		
Protein	34	141	34%

Quick & Easy Tip:

If you have leftover steak from this meal, use it the next morning in a **Breakfast Burrito** (page 30).

BARBECUED TACO SALAD

Time in the Kitchen: 30 minutes
Servings: 3

2 hearts of Romaine or cos, quartered lengthways

2 tomatoes, cut into chunks

1 red or white onion, cut into chunks

1 green pepper, cut into chunks

2 avocados (not overly ripe), peeled, stoned and cut in half

2 tablespoons of oil, plus more for coating vegetables

450 g (1 lb) skirt steak

½ teaspoon cumin

¼ teaspoon paprika

¼ teaspoon chilli powder

¼ teaspoon salt

If you're really in a hurry you can simply grill the steak and throw the rest of these ingredients into a bowl raw, but taking a little extra time to barbecue everything creates a unique meal. Romaine and avocado take on a subtle smoky flavour when barbecued and are worth trying if you've only ever eaten them raw.

Heat the barbecue to medium-high heat.

Drizzle oil over the Romaine hearts and vegetables, giving them a light but thorough coating. The tomato, onion, pepper and avocado can be cooked in a grilling basket or put on skewers. If skewering, put only one type of vegetable on each skewer so you can remove the skewers from the grill as each item finishes cooking (for example, you'll want to remove the avocado and tomato skewers from the grill before the onion and green pepper).

Mix 2 tablespoons of oil with the spices and salt and thoroughly coat skirt steak.

Put the skirt steak on the barbecue and spread the vegetable skewers and Romaine evenly around it. Close the lid and grill for 3 minutes, then flip the skirt steak and Romaine quarters and turn the skewers.

Close the lid for another three minutes, then remove the steak (for rare) or barbecue another 2–3 minutes for medium. The avocado, tomatoes and romaine can also be removed after a total of 6–8 minutes on the grill. The onion and peppers can stay on longer, until they are lightly charred.

Slice the steak thinly and cut the romaine into bite-sized chunks. Toss with avocado, tomato and onions. Add salt to taste and garnish with a wedge of lime and chopped coriander. Serve immediately.

Macronutrient Profile (per serving)

	Grams	Calories	%-Cals
Calories		737	
Fat	49	422	57%
Saturated	11	100	14%
Polyunsaturated	5	41	6%
Monounsaturated	29	252	34%
Carbohydrate	34	123	17%
Dietary Fibre	20		
Protein	49	194	26%

GREEK SALAD WITH LAMB

Time in the Kitchen: 20 minutes
Servings: 3

450 g (1 lb) lamb mince

25 g (1 oz) Greek herbs such as dill, mint, oregano, parsley, finely chopped

salt to taste

2 hearts of Romaine or cos lettuce, finely chopped

1–2 tomatoes, chopped

1 large or 2–4 small cucumbers, chopped

175 g (6 oz) stoned Kalamata or other Greek olives

60 ml (2 fl oz) lemon juice

125 ml (4fl oz) olive oil

A traditional Greek salad includes cucumbers, peppers, olives, tomatoes and fresh herbs, but I can't think of a good reason not to add meat, too. What better meat to add to a Greek-inspired dish than lamb? Lamb mince turns this light salad into a substantial meal.

Sauté lamb mince with herbs for 6–8 minutes, or until cooked through. Add salt to taste.

Combine meat with lettuce, tomato, cucumber and olives.

Whisk together lemon juice and olive oil. Drizzle on top of salad.

Macronutrient Profile (per serving)

	Grams	Calories	%-Cals
Calories		911	
Fat	72	641	70%
Saturated	18	161	18%
Polyunsaturated	7	62	7%
Monounsaturated	43	376	41%
Carbohydrate	26	92	10%
Dietary Fibre	13		
Protein	45	179	20%

PORK AND SHIITAKE LETTUCE CUPS

Time in the Kitchen: 20 minutes
Servings: 2–4 *(macronutrient profile based on 4 servings)*

3 large shiitake mushrooms, thinly sliced

450 g (1 lb) pork mince

3 spring onions, chopped

2 tablespoons tamari

2 tablespoons fish sauce

15 g (½ oz) fresh mint, roughly chopped

1 head of iceberg or Romaine lettuce

juice of 1 lime, plus wedges to garnish

So much flavour with so few ingredients... that's what I love about this quick lunch (which also makes a great starter). This recipe is a simplified version of a Thai salad called Larb, often served with minced chicken or beef. Whichever type of meat you choose, just don't forget the fresh lime at the end; it heightens the flavour of each bite.

Sauté mushrooms for several minutes, then add pork. When pork is almost cooked through, add spring onions, tamari and fish sauce.

Sauté until pork is done. Add mint. Scoop into iceberg lettuce leaves and serve with wedges of lime.

Macronutrient Profile (per serving)

	Grams	Calories	%-Cals
Calories		378	
Fat	24	216	57%
Saturated	9	80	21%
Polyunsaturated	2	21	6%
Monounsaturated	11	95	25%
Carbohydrate	8	28	7%
Dietary Fibre	3		
Protein	33	135	36%

Quick & Easy Tip:

If you're trying to cut back on salt, the easiest way to heighten the flavour in a dish is with a squirt of acidity. Lemon, lime or vinegar will make flavour come alive—this recipe is a perfect example!

DILL AND CAPER SALMON BURGERS

Time in the Kitchen: 30 minutes
Servings: 4

675 g (1½ lb) skinless, boneless wild salmon

2 teaspoons Dijon mustard

2 tablespoons dill, finely chopped

1 tablespoon capers, drained

1 jalapeño or green chilli, seeds and white veins removed, finely chopped

2 tablespoons finely chopped red onion

¼ teaspoon salt

lemon, cut into wedges, for garnish

You'll have no trouble forming these flavourful salmon burgers into patties without needless fillers like breadcrumbs or egg. Once you master this version, be creative with how you flavour the salmon burgers. Try spring onions, ginger and tamari, or black olives and basil.

To save time, ask your fishmonger to skin and de-bone the salmon for you.

Cut the salmon into chunks and put ¼ of it in the food processor with the mustard. Pulse until the salmon forms a smooth paste. It is this paste-like texture that will help the burgers hold together. Add the remaining salmon and ingredients and pulse to break the salmon up into small chunks, but not so long that it becomes smooth.

Shape the salmon into four burgers. The burgers can be fried in a frying pan with a little oil, grilled, or barbecued. In both cases, cook for 3–5 minutes until the burger is firm and easy to flip. Continue cooking the second side for another 3–5 minutes. Serve with wedges of lemon.

Macronutrient Profile (per serving)

	Grams	Calories	%-Cals
Calories		320	
Fat	13	116	36%
Saturated	3	25	8%
Polyunsaturated	4	39	12%
Monounsaturated	5	42	13%
Carbohydrate	1	5	1%
Dietary Fibre	0		
Protein	47	200	62%

BLTA CHICKEN BREAST SANDWICH

Time in the Kitchen: 25 minutes
Servings: 1

1 chicken breast, preferably skin on

1 tablespoon mayonnaise

2 slices of cooked bacon

1 handful of rocket or lettuce

1 tomato, thinly sliced

1 avocado, thinly sliced

After one bite of this sandwich, you'll wonder why you ever thought you needed two slices of bread to hold a sandwich together. Pure protein and flavour is what this sandwich is all about. Although you can eat it with a knife and fork if you want, it is a sandwich after all, so don't be afraid to simply pick it up and take a bite.

Butterfly the chicken breast by cutting lengthways through the middle of the breast without cutting all the way through, so it can be opened up. Lightly salt and pepper the chicken breast.

Heat a little oil in a pan and sear the chicken breast, skin side down and opened up. Cook 4–6 minutes on the first side until nicely browned, then flip the chicken and cook the other side with a lid on the pan for a further 6–10 minutes, depending on the thickness of the chicken breast.

When chicken is cooked, spread a thin layer of mayonnaise on the inside. Layer bacon, lettuce, tomato and avocado and fold the chicken breast shut. Eat warm or cold.

Macronutrient Profile (per serving)

	Grams	Calories	%-Cals
Calories		878	
Fat	60	518	59%
Saturated	12	101	12%
Polyunsaturated	13	117	13%
Monounsaturated	30	259	29%
Carbohydrate	22	80	9%
Dietary Fibre	15		
Protein	67	280	32%

CHICKEN EGG DROP SOUP

Time in the Kitchen: 15 minutes
Servings: 3–4 *(macronutrient profile based on 4 servings)*

1 litre (1¾ pints) chicken stock

225 g (8 oz) chicken breast, cut into thin strips

130–260 g (4½–9¼ oz) chopped fresh vegetables or frozen vegetables (broccoli, green beans, carrots etc, chopped)

2 eggs, beaten

2–3 spring onions or salad onions, sliced

Drizzling egg into hot broth creates a dumpling-like texture that makes a simple bowl of chicken soup a lot heartier. Egg drop soup is often served in Chinese restaurants, and you can easily give this soup even more of an Asian flair by adding sliced mushrooms and drizzling a little tamari and sesame oil into the broth.

Bring chicken stock to a gentle boil. Add raw chicken and raw vegetables. Simmer rapidly for five minutes.

Pour eggs into the stock in a steady stream, then gently stir the broth while the egg cooks.

Remove from heat after a minute or two and garnish with spring onions or salad onions.

Macronutrient Profile (per serving)

	Grams	Calories	%-Cals
Calories		192	
Fat	6	50	27%
Saturated	2	15	8%
Polyunsaturated	1	10	5%
Monounsaturated	2	19	10%
Carbohydrate	14	54	28%
Dietary Fibre	4		
Protein	20	85	45%

SPINACH COCONUT MILK SOUP WITH CURRIED PRAWNS

Time in the Kitchen: 15 minutes
Servings: 3

2   cans coconut milk

156 g (5½ oz) frozen spinach, or several handfuls of fresh

1   tablespoon butter

450 g (1 lb) raw prawns, peeled and deveined

1½ teaspoons curry powder

   salt to taste

It doesn't get much easier than this soup. The spinach and coconut milk purée has such a great flavour and texture that you don't even need to add broth. When you have more time use this recipe as a starting point, then add more ingredients to the soup like diced vegetables, additional spices and more seafood.

In a blender, purée coconut milk and spinach until smooth.

In a deep saucepan, melt the butter. Add the prawns and sprinkle curry powder on top. Sauté 2 minutes, then add coconut milk with spinach. Bring to the boil then turn off heat. Salt to taste and serve.

Macronutrient Profile (per serving)

	Grams	Calories	%-Cals
Calories		529	
Fat	36	305	58%
Saturated	28	237	45%
Polyunsaturated	2	17	3%
Monounsaturated	3	24	4%
Carbohydrate	10	37	7%
Dietary Fibre	3		
Protein	46	188	35%

PORK CHOPS WITH SHREDDED BRUSSELS SPROUTS

Time in the Kitchen: 25 minutes
Servings: 2

450 g (1 lb) Brussels sprouts
60–125 ml (2–4 fl oz) olive oil
2 thin pork chops
salt and pepper to taste

When Brussels sprouts are shredded, they magically transform into a whole new thing. Try this dish on your pickiest vegetable eater and see if they even notice they're eating a vegetable they claim to dislike. (Grating a little cheese on top will make the dish especially appealing to kids.)

Trim the bottom stem off each Brussels sprout. Grate the sprouts in the food processor. Set aside.

Lightly salt and pepper the pork chops. Over a medium-high heat, heat a few tablespoons of oil, waiting until pan is nice and hot before adding chops. Cook the pork chops 4 minutes on each side to brown, then if needed add a lid and cook about 4 minutes more or until they reach desired doneness.

While pork chops are cooking, warm 60 ml (2 fl oz) of olive oil over a medium-high heat. Add the shredded Brussels sprouts and sauté until softened and lightly browned, about 10 minutes. As the Brussels sprouts cook, add more oil as needed. Salt and pepper to taste.

Macronutrient Profile (per serving)

	Grams	Calories	%-Cals
Calories		756	
Fat	66	584	77%
Saturated	12	104	14%
Polyunsaturated	7	63	8%
Monounsaturated	44	393	52%
Carbohydrate	16	57	8%
Dietary Fibre	6		
Protein	29	115	15%

PORK LOIN SALAD WITH DATE VINAIGRETTE

Time in the Kitchen: 20 minutes
Servings: 2

225 g (8 oz) pork loin
4 dates, stoned
6 anchovy fillets
grated zest of 1 large lemon
2 garlic cloves
90 ml (3 fl oz) olive oil
1 tablespoon sherry vinegar
1 fennel bulb
4 handfuls of mixed lettuce

In this recipe a surprising combination of ingredients come together in an unforgettable way, resulting in a sweet, salty and garlicky salad that's downright addictive.

Slice the pork loin into rounds no more than 2.5-cm (1-in) thick. Lightly salt and pepper the meat and set aside.

In a food processor or blender, process dates, anchovies, lemon zest, garlic cloves, olive oil and vinegar until blended as much as possible. The vinaigrette will have a thick, chunky texture.

Remove the stem and fronds from the fennel and cut the bulb in half, removing the inner core. Slice each half into very thin strips. If you have a mandoline, use it to slice the fennel paper-thin.

Heat a few tablespoons of olive oil in a frying pan over a medium heat. Add the fennel, sautéing until lightly browned, about 3 minutes for slightly crunchy fennel, longer to soften the texture and make the flavour milder.

Add the pork and as the first side cooks, spread about a teaspoon of the vinaigrette onto each piece. After three minutes, flip the pork medallions and cook just a few minutes more, so the outside of the meat is browned but the inside is still a bit pink.

Toss the lettuce with the remaining vinaigrette and divide on two plates. Top with the fennel and pork.

Macronutrient Profile (per serving)

	Grams	Calories	%-Cals
Calories		702	
Fat	43	379	54%
Saturated	7	64	9%
Polyunsaturated	5	42	6%
Monounsaturated	29	254	36%
Carbohydrate	45	161	23%
Dietary Fibre	7		
Protein	39	160	23%

PORK FRIED CAULIFLOWER RICE

Time in the Kitchen: 15 minutes
Servings: 2–3 *(macronutrient profile based on 3 servings)*

3 tablespoons sesame or coconut oil (coconut oil will give the dish coconut flavour)

1 white or yellow onion, thinly sliced

350 g (12 oz) meat, raw or already cooked, cut into small pieces

4 tablespoons tamari

1 garlic clove, finely chopped

1 small head of cauliflower, grated in a food processor

2 eggs, beaten

115 g (4 oz) frozen peas

4 spring onions, roughly chopped

Fried cauliflower rice is the perfect dish when you have leftover meat in the fridge, either raw or already cooked. Pork, chicken, steak, prawns... all will blend right in with the simple flavours of garlic and tamari. This fried cauliflower rice cooks so quickly, you'll never miss takeaway fried rice again.

Heat a wok or frying pan over a high heat and add 1 tablespoon of oil. Add onion and sauté until it starts to brown, about 2 minutes.

Add the meat and 1 tablespoon of tamari. Sauté 2–3 minutes (or longer if raw meat needs more time) then add the remaining oil, the garlic and the cauliflower. Sauté 2–3 minutes.

Add the eggs and remaining tamari. Stir constantly as the egg cooks, then add peas and chopped spring onions. Cook just a minute or two more.

Macronutrient Profile *(per serving)*

	Grams	Calories	%-Cals
Calories		521	
Fat	26	227	44%
Saturated	6	51	10%
Polyunsaturated	7	64	12%
Monounsaturated	10	89	17%
Carbohydrate	18	71	14%
Dietary Fibre	6		
Protein	54	222	43%

SPICE-RUBBED BARBECUED PORK AND CARROTS

Time in the Kitchen: 25 minutes
Servings: 2

3 tablespoons butter

1 teaspoon chilli powder

1 teaspoon cumin

½ teaspoon cinnamon

½ teaspoon salt

2 2.5-cm (1-in) thick pork chops

8 carrots, peeled and cut in half lengthways

Chilli powder mixed with cinnamon and cumin creates a subtly sweet and smoky flavour combination. Carrots aren't often barbecued, but it's really the perfect cooking method for this vegetable. The flames caramelize the carrots' flavour just a bit and the texture turns tender without being mushy.

Heat the barbecue to medium-high heat.

Melt the butter and mix in spices and salt. Drizzle half the butter mixture over the carrots, tossing the carrots with your hands to make sure they are thoroughly covered. Brush the remaining butter over both sides of the pork chops.

Char pork chops and carrots for five minutes on each side, then move them away from direct heat (with charcoal) or turn the heat to medium (gas barbecue) and cover the barbecue for a further three minutes. The carrots are probably fairly tender at this point and can be removed from the grill. The pork may need a few minutes more.

Sprinkle pork and carrots with sea salt to finish.

Macronutrient Profile (per serving)

	Grams	Calories	%-Cals
Calories		437	
Fat	29	256	58%
Saturated	15	133	30%
Polyunsaturated	2	16	4%
Monounsaturated	10	85	19%
Carbohydrate	20	75	17%
Dietary Fibre	8		
Protein	26	107	24%

Quick & Easy Tip:

Leftover pork from dinner? Use it to make **Pork Fried Cauliflower Rice** (page 100) tomorrow for lunch.

UN-STUFFED CABBAGE

Time in the Kitchen: 30 minutes
Servings: 4

1 small white or yellow onion, finely chopped or grated

2 large turnips, grated (a head of grated cauliflower can be used instead)

225 g (8 oz) pork mince

225 g (8 oz) lean beef mince

1 teaspoon salt

½ teaspoon black pepper

1 tablespoon dried parsley

1 400 g (14 oz) can diced tomatoes in juice (or several fresh tomatoes)

1 head green cabbage

Stuffed cabbage is a comfort dish many of us don't eat as often as we'd like simply because it takes so much time to stuff those darn cabbage leaves. This method is much faster and tastes just as good, even though I serve the cabbage un-stuffed and substitute grated turnip for rice.

In a deep pot over a medium-high heat, sauté onion and turnip for a few minutes, then cover with a lid and cook for three minutes to steam the turnip.

Remove the lid and add minced meats, salt, pepper and parsley. Sauté for 6–8 minutes then add the can of tomatoes. Simmer rapidly for 10 minutes, stirring occasionally.

While the meat is simmering, cut the cabbage into quarters, removing inner core. Separate leaves slightly then microwave cabbage leaves, covered with a loose lid, for 5 minutes. Flavour with a little butter and salt.

Serve the minced meat and turnip with a side of cabbage.

Macronutrient Profile (per serving)

	Grams	Calories	%-Cals
Calories		398	
Fat	21	187	47%
Saturated	8	73	18%
Polyunsaturated	2	15	4%
Monounsaturated	9	78	20%
Carbohydrate	22	81	20%
Dietary Fibre	7		
Protein	33	131	33%

SAUTÉED SAUERKRAUT WITH SAUSAGE AND COURGETTE

Time in the Kitchen: 15 minutes
Servings: 2

2 sausages, sliced

2 small or 1 large courgette, sliced or finely chopped

1 red pepper, sliced or finely chopped

284 g (10 oz) sauerkraut

Sausage and sauerkraut are a classic combination. In this recipe, I simply forgo the bun and sauté the two together. If you like, serve mustard on the side for dipping.

Sauté sausage in a pan over a medium heat until browned and heated through.

Add more oil to the pan if needed and sauté courgette and red pepper for about five minutes.

Add sauerkraut and sauté until heated.

Macronutrient Profile (per serving)

	Grams	Calories	%-Cals
Calories		138	
Fat	5	43	31%
Saturated	1	13	9%
Polyunsaturated	1	9	6%
Monounsaturated	2	15	11%
Carbohydrate	21	75	54%
Dietary Fibre	8		
Protein	7	21	15%

CREAMY SAUERKRAUT AND SAUSAGE SOUP

Time in the Kitchen: 30 minutes
Servings: 2–4 *(macronutrient profile based on 4 servings)*

- 2 tablespoons butter
- 225 g (8 oz) sausage, sliced
- 80 g (3 oz) white onion, chopped
- 236g (8⅓ oz) sauerkraut, rinsed and drained
- 90 ml (3 fl oz) dry white wine
- 600 ml (1 pint) chicken stock
- 60 ml (2 fl oz) double cream
- 2 teaspoons Dijon mustard

Sausage, sauerkraut and mustard are a natural combination, although you may be surprised to find out how well they come together in a soup. The fermented, sour flavour of the kraut is mellowed by the creamy broth but still has a little kick that brings out the best in the sausage.

In a deep pot over a medium heat, melt 1 tablespoon of butter and cook the sausage until browned. Remove sausage from pot and set aside.

Add remaining butter and the onion and cook until soft. Add sauerkraut and wine and keep at a rapid boil for five minutes.

Turn heat down slightly and add stock. Simmer uncovered for 10 minutes.

Remove from heat and stir in double cream and mustard. Purée the soup in small batches in a blender until smooth and creamy. Return the soup to the pot and add the sausage. Season with salt and pepper.

Macronutrient Profile (per serving)

	Grams	Calories	%-Cals
Calories		377	
Fat	32	288	77%
Saturated	14	124	33%
Polyunsaturated	3	31	8%
Monounsaturated	12	109	29%
Carbohydrate	6	22	6%
Dietary Fibre	1		
Protein	12	52	14%

Quick & Easy Tip:

If you're using just a little bit of cream in a recipe, freeze the rest in small portions for future recipes. Kept in airtight containers, the frozen cream will keep about 4 months in the freezer and can be easily reheated for future recipes without losing its flavour or texture.

CAULIFLOWER 'ARROZ CON POLLO'

Time in the Kitchen: 30 minutes
Servings: 4

1 tablespoon oil

900 g–1.1 kg (2–2½ lb) boneless chicken thighs, cut into small cubes or strips (breast meat can also be used, but isn't as moist)

1 onion, finely chopped

1 jalapeño or green chilli, finely chopped

2 garlic cloves, finely chopped

1 green pepper, chopped or cut into strips

1 red pepper, chopped or cut into strips

1 400 g (14 oz) can diced tomatoes

225 ml (8 fl oz) chicken stock

½ teaspoon saffron threads

1 teaspoon cumin

1 teaspoon salt

1 head cauliflower, grated

230 g (8 oz) frozen peas

Rice with chicken is a simple but popular dish in many cultures. Surprisingly, substituting grated cauliflower in for the rice hardly changes how the dish tastes. Because cauliflower does not soak up liquid as well as rice, this version will have a little more broth than traditional *Arroz con Pollo*, but the flavour is still fantastic.

If you have a food processor, save time by using it to grate or slice the onion, jalapeño, garlic and peppers together. The cauliflower is also easiest to grate in a food processor.

In a deep saucepan, heat oil over a medium-high and add chicken. Cook for 4–6 minutes until nicely browned. Add more oil if needed, then add onion, garlic, jalapeño and peppers for several minutes.

Add tomatoes and their juice, stock, saffron, cumin, salt and cauliflower. Stir well. Simmer rapidly with lid on for 10 minutes, then add peas and simmer a few more minutes.

Macronutrient Profile (per serving)

	Grams	Calories	%-Cals
Calories		839	
Fat	48	432	52%
Saturated	13	116	14%
Polyunsaturated	10	93	11%
Monounsaturated	20	180	21%
Carbohydrate	23	85	10%
Dietary Fibre	6		
Protein	77	321	38%

CHICKEN AND ARTICHOKES WITH GARLIC SAUCE

Time in the Kitchen: 25 minutes
Servings: 4

90 ml (3 fl oz) olive oil

3 tablespoons butter

6 preserved anchovy fillets (sold jarred in supermarkets)

4 garlic cloves, finely chopped

zest of 2 small or 1 large lemon

900 g (2 lb) chicken, cut into 2.5-cm (1-in) chunks

2 400 g (14 oz) cans of artichoke hearts, drained and quartered

15 g (½ oz) parsley, roughly chopped

If you want to feel like a gourmet cook without much effort, this is the recipe to serve. Buttery and richly flavoured without being too heavy, you'll want to lick up every last bit on your plate. If by chance there are any leftovers, the chicken and artichokes make a great salad topping for lunch the next day.

In a frying pan over a medium heat combine the olive oil, butter and anchovies. As the butter melts, smash the anchovies into a paste with a wooden spoon. When the anchovies have dissolved and the butter and oil is bubbling, turn off the heat and mix in garlic and lemon zest.

Turn the grill on high.

Combine the chicken and artichokes in a rimmed baking tin. Sprinkle lightly with salt and pepper. Drizzle the oil mixture on top and mix well to coat.

Cook the chicken for 10–15 minutes, stirring several times until done.

Garnish with parsley and serve.

Macronutrient Profile (per serving)

	Grams	Calories	%-Cals
Calories		872	
Fat	61	540	62%
Saturated	17	153	18%
Polyunsaturated	10	89	10%
Monounsaturated	29	256	29%
Carbohydrate	14	52	6%
Dietary Fibre	7		
Protein	68	281	32%

VEGETABLE COCONUT STEW

Time in the Kitchen: 20 minutes
Servings: 4

1 large shallot, roughly chopped

80 g (3 oz) coconut flakes

2 garlic cloves

1 jalapeño or green chilli, deseeded and cut in half

2 tablespoons coconut oil

1 large cucumber or several small cucumbers, peeled, deseeded and sliced

1 small head of cauliflower, broken into florets

1 carrot, peeled and cut into rounds

370 g (13 oz) green beans

2 tomatoes, chopped

1 teaspoon turmeric

½ teaspoon cumin

350 ml (12 fl oz) coconut milk (canned)

salt to taste

125 ml (4 fl oz) full fat Greek-style yogurt (optional)

This stew of crisp vegetables in coconut broth is especially nice in the summer. Green beans, tomatoes and even cucumber, which is surprisingly delicious when cooked, are simmered briefly to retain their flavour and texture. The bright yellow colour of the broth comes from turmeric, a spice related to ginger that is known for its anti-inflammatory properties.

If you'd like to add meat to this stew, simply sauté it first, then start adding the vegetables.

In a food processor, combine shallot, coconut flakes, garlic and jalapeño for about one minute until very finely shredded.

In a deep saucepan, warm coconut oil and add the shallot mixture to the pan. Sauté several minutes.

Add cucumber, cauliflower, carrot, green beans, tomato, turmeric and cumin. Sauté a minute or two then add coconut milk and bring to a rapid simmer. Cover and cook 8–10 minutes until vegetables are cooked, but still a bit crisp.

Add salt to taste. If using the yogurt, which will make the broth thick and creamy, stir in right before serving.

Macronutrient Profile (per serving)

	Grams	Calories	%-Cals
Calories		738	
Fat	67	563	76%
Saturated	59	493	67%
Polyunsaturated	1	9	1%
Monounsaturated	3	25	3%
Carbohydrate	37	142	19%
Dietary Fibre	17		
Protein	11	33	4%

COURGETTE CARBONARA

Time in the Kitchen: 20 minutes
Servings: 2

6 small or 4 large courgettes

2 egg yolks, beaten

60 ml (2 fl oz) double cream or coconut milk

½ teaspoon black pepper

125 g (4 oz) pancetta (or bacon) cut into small pieces

finely chopped parsley or basil to garnish

olive oil for sautéing

salt to taste

Traditional Italian *Pasta alla Carbonara* combines pasta with a lip-smacking sauce of cream, barely cooked egg yolks, parmigiano-reggiano cheese and pancetta. Following the Italians' lead, I've kept the sauce (minus the cheese, but you can add a handful if you like) and used it to smother courgette 'noodles' instead of starchy pasta.

To make wide pappardelle noodles, slice each courgette lengthways into slices that are as thin as possible. The easiest way to slice the courgette this thinly is on a mandoline. If you don't have a mandoline, just use a knife and do your best.

Whisk together egg yolks, cream/coconut milk and pepper. Set aside.

Heat two frying pans over a medium heat. In one, heat several tablespoons of olive oil and add courgettes. Sauté for about five minutes until just soft and lightly browned.

Simultaneously in the second pan, cook pancetta until crispy. Spoon the cooked pancetta into the bowl with the eggs then drizzle the mixture on top of the courgettes.

Stir while the heat gently warms and thickens the sauce. Make sure to remove from heat before eggs take on a scrambled look.

Garnish with parsley or basil and salt to taste.

Macronutrient Profile (per serving)

	Grams	Calories	%-Cals
Calories		849	
Fat	63	557	65%
Saturated	20	176	21%
Polyunsaturated	7	64	7%
Monounsaturated	31	273	32%
Carbohydrate	47	167	20%
Dietary Fibre	14		
Protein	34	127	15%

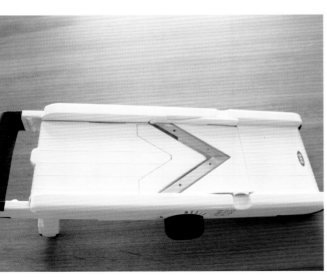

COD AND ARAME WITH LEMON TAMARI DRESSING

Time in the Kitchen: 20 minutes
Servings: 2

100 g (3½ oz) dried arame

450 g (1 lb) cod

2 tablespoons sesame oil, plus 60 ml (2 fl oz)

2 garlic cloves, finely chopped

3 tablespoons lemon juice

1 teaspoon tamari

3 spring onions, chopped

Arame is thought to have the mildest flavour of all the dried sea vegetables and a cooked texture that is similar to wild rice. Like most sea vegetables, arame is a highly concentrated source of nutrients. It is a tasty bed on which to lay fish, like cod.

Bring a medium saucepan of water to the boil and preheat grill to high.

Add arame to boiling water and boil for 10 minutes. Drain and rinse.

Pat cod fillets dry then lightly salt and pepper. Cover with 2 tablespoons of sesame oil and garlic. Grill for 8–10 minutes. When the cod is done, the fish will flake apart easily.

Whisk together the remaining sesame oil with lemon juice and tamari.

Toss the dressing with the arame. Divide the arame on two plates and top with cod and spring onions.

Macronutrient Profile (per serving)

	Grams	Calories	%-Cals
Calories		678	
Fat	49	437	64%
Saturated	7	65	10%
Polyunsaturated	20	174	26%
Monounsaturated	20	173	25%
Carbohydrate	9	31	5%
Dietary Fibre	1		
Protein	51	211	31%

THAI-INSPIRED SCALLOP SOUP

Time in the Kitchen: 20 minutes
Servings: 3

1 tablespoon butter

1 tablespoon finely chopped fresh ginger

2 garlic cloves, crushed

225 g (8 oz) scallops

1 can (400 ml/14 fl oz) coconut milk

500 ml (18 fl oz) chicken stock

1 red or orange pepper, cut into thin strips

2 spring onions, thinly sliced

60 ml (2 fl oz) freshly squeezed lime juice

15 g (½ oz) basil, finely chopped

This is a simplified version of the Tom Kha soup with coconut broth that is served at many Thai restaurants. Lime juice is a key ingredient in the soup, adding a refreshing and tart flavour that balances the richness of the coconut milk. Prawns can be used in place of the scallops and if you like it spicy, go ahead and add hot chilli sauce at the end.

Heat butter in a deep saucepan over a medium heat. Add ginger and garlic and sauté briefly.

Lightly salt scallops then add them to the pan. Sauté 2–3 minutes then add coconut milk, chicken stock, pepper and spring onions.

Bring the soup to a gentle boil then remove from heat and stir in lime juice and basil.

Add salt or hot sauce to taste.

Macronutrient Profile (per serving)

	Grams	Calories	%-Cals
Calories		459	
Fat	38	319	70%
Saturated	30	253	55%
Polyunsaturated	2	13	3%
Monounsaturated	4	31	7%
Carbohydrate	16	59	13%
Dietary Fibre	4		
Protein	20	79	17%

HALIBUT IN BUTTER SAUCE

Time in the Kitchen: 20 minutes
Servings: 2

450 g (1 lb) halibut, about 2.5-cm (1-in) thick

6 tablespoons butter

1 shallot, finely chopped

125 ml (4 fl oz) dry white wine

125 ml (4 fl oz) vegetable or chicken stock

1 tablespoon finely chopped parsley

1 lemon

The rich, meaty texture of halibut has a natural affinity for butter, although any type of white fish will be elevated by this simple sauce. After making this dish once you might even be tempted to double the amount of sauce served with the fish, and I can't blame you. There's something about melted butter that's hard to resist.

Pat halibut dry and lightly season with salt and pepper. Heat 1 tablespoon of butter in a frying pan over a medium heat and add halibut.

After about 2 minutes the butter will begin to brown; add another tablespoon of butter and the shallot.

Add the wine and turn the heat up slightly, simmering rapidly for three minutes. Add chicken stock and continue simmering for 4–5 more minutes, spooning some of the broth over the fish.

Reduce the heat to medium-low and stir in the parsley. Add the remaining butter in small chunks. Put a lid on the frying pan and simmer for 3–6 minutes until the halibut is cooked through and flakes apart easily. Serve with a wedge of lemon.

Macronutrient Profile (per serving)

	Grams	Calories	%-Cals
Calories		682	
Fat	41	365	53%
Saturated	23	201	29%
Polyunsaturated	3	31	5%
Monounsaturated	11	99	14%
Carbohydrate	3	13	2%
Dietary Fibre	0		
Protein	62	263	39%

SEAFOOD SOUP WITH TOMATO BROTH

Time in the Kitchen: 30 minutes
Servings: 4

1 white or yellow onion, chopped

1 fennel bulb, thinly sliced

4 garlic cloves, finely chopped

225 ml (8 fl oz) white wine

360 g (12¾ oz) fresh tomatoes, chopped or 1 (400g/14 oz) can diced tomatoes in juice

600 ml (1 pint) fish or chicken stock

450 g (1 lb) mussels, scrubbed well

225 g (8 oz) clams, scrubbed well

450 g (1 lb) white fish (try cod or halibut)

225 g (8 oz) scallops

salt and pepper to taste

basil or parsley to garnish

This soup is commonly referred to as Cioppino, and it doesn't need a lot of time on the hob to develop flavour. The real key to great cioppino is adding lots of seafood, so don't hold back – just make sure to use a large pot.

In a few tablespoons of butter or olive oil, sauté onion and fennel until soft, about five minutes.

Add garlic, then wine and bring to the boil.

Add tomatoes and stock. Boil for 10 minutes, stirring occasionally.

Add seafood and stir so all the seafood is mostly covered by broth. Cover and cook until the clams and mussels begin to open, about 5 minutes. Add salt and pepper to taste. Garnish with chopped parsley or basil and serve.

Macronutrient Profile (per serving)

	Grams	Calories	%-Cals
Calories		501	
Fat	10	93	19%
Saturated	2	16	3%
Polyunsaturated	3	27	5%
Monounsaturated	3	24	5%
Carbohydrate	24	92	18%
Dietary Fibre	2		
Protein	65	273	55%

CHORIZO AND ALMOND-CRUSTED HALIBUT

Time in the Kitchen: 25 minutes
Servings: 2

55 g (2 oz) roughly chopped Spanish chorizo (cured salami, not raw sausages)

40 g (1½ oz) blanched almonds with no skin

1 tablespoon roughly chopped parsley

2 skinned halibut fillets (or other white fish), about 225 g (8 oz) each

The meaty, salty and slightly spicy flavour of chorizo gives more flavour to mild fish like halibut, and blending almonds into the topping adds a nice crunch to the dish. While almonds pair well with the chorizo, there's no reason you can't experiment with other nuts, too.

Preheat oven to 200°C/400°F/Gas Mark 6.

In a blender, blend the chorizo, almonds and parsley until almonds are in small pieces.

Drizzle a few tablespoons of olive oil in the bottom of a pan and set the fish on top. Spoon the chorizo mixture on top of the fish, patting it down so it sticks as much as possible and the sides are partially covered.

Roast in the oven for 12 minutes, or until the fish flakes easily with a fork. To finish, turn the grill to high and grill for 2–4 minutes until the nuts are lightly browned.

Macronutrient Profile (per serving)

	Grams	Calories	%-Cals
Calories		582	
Fat	29	258	44%
Saturated	7	60	10%
Polyunsaturated	6	49	8%
Monounsaturated	15	127	22%
Carbohydrate	4	17	3%
Dietary Fibre	2		
Protein	73	309	53%

KOREAN CAULIFLOWER RICE BOWL

Time in the Kitchen: 30 minutes
Servings: 2

4   garlic cloves, finely chopped

125 ml (4 fl oz) tamari

2   tablespoons unseasoned rice wine vinegar

60 ml (2 fl oz) toasted sesame oil

about half a head of cauliflower, grated

2   carrots, grated or very thinly sliced

156 g (5½ oz) frozen spinach or 2 large handfuls fresh spinach

2   eggs

225g (8 oz) sirloin or flank steak, thinly sliced

3   fresh shiitake mushrooms, sliced

Optional garnishes:

1   sheet dried seaweed (nori), cut into thin strips

1   tablespoon sesame seeds, lightly toasted

3   sping onions, chopped

This is a Primal version of Korean Bi Bim Bap, a traditional rice bowl filled with numerous ingredients that all add a specific flavour and texture. Cooking each ingredient separately allows the uniqueness of each to stand alone in the dish; if you're in a huge hurry, you can throw the veggies and meat into the pan together, but the final result will taste slightly different.

Mix together garlic, tamari, vinegar and sesame oil. Place beef and mushrooms in separate bowls and pour half of the marinade in each bowl.

Heat the grated cauliflower in the microwave for 2–4 minutes until soft. Separate into two bowls.

Heat a tablespoon of oil (sesame, coconut or olive oil) in a wok or large frying pan. As you sauté each ingredient, add more oil as needed. When each ingredient finishes cooking, split it between the two bowls of cauliflower rice.

Sauté the carrots for a few minutes until lightly browned. Remove from frying pan. Add the spinach to the pan and sauté until warm. Remove from pan.

Crack eggs in the pan, frying until whites are set and yolk reaches desired firmness. Remove from pan. Eggs can be left whole, or if the yolk is firm, cut into slices.

Bring the heat back up to high and add a little oil to the frying pan. Remove beef from marinade (reserving marinade in the bowl) and sauté until the beef is cooked through, 3–5 minutes. Remove from pan.

Take mushrooms out of the marinade and sauté until soft. Remove from pan. Pour the leftover meat marinade into the pan and bring to a gentle boil for 3 minutes.

Pour marinade over each rice bowl to taste. Add optional garnishes of dried seaweed, sesame seeds and scallions.

Macronutrient Profile (per serving)

	Grams	Calories	%-Cals
Calories		710	
Fat	46	409	58%
Saturated	10	91	13%
Polyunsaturated	13	119	17%
Monounsaturated	18	159	22%
Carbohydrate	24	89	13%
Dietary Fibre	11		
Protein	54	211	30%

SPAGHETTI SQUASH WITH BEEF RAGU

Time in the Kitchen: 30 minutes
Servings: 4

2 tomatoes

3–4 roasted red peppers

12.5–25 g ($\frac{1}{3}$–1 oz) fresh basil, roughly chopped

60 ml (2 fl oz) olive oil

1 onion, finely chopped

3 garlic cloves, finely chopped

450 g (1 lb) lean mince beef

1 spaghetti squash

Spaghetti squash is available year-round and as the name suggests, is the perfect substitution for pasta. Topped with a quick but flavourful sauce, it's a meal the whole family will love. A traditional ragu can take hours to develop flavour, but I cheat a bit by throwing in roasted red peppers, which adds sweetness to mellow the acidity of tomatoes.

Cut tomatoes in half or quarters and put them in a food processor or blender with roasted red peppers and basil, until the sauce reaches the texture you desire (either slightly chunky or totally smooth).

In a deep saucepan over a medium-high heat, warm the olive oil. Add onion and sauté 1–2 minutes, then add garlic and beef mince. Season beef with salt and pepper and cook 4–5 minutes until beef is lightly browned but still slightly pink, then add the tomato and red pepper purée. Turn heat to high and simmer rapidly for 10 minutes.

While the sauce is simmering, cut the spaghetti squash in half and scoop out the seeds and stringy pulp. Microwave each half 6–8 minutes, until soft. Scrape out noodle-like insides with a fork, drizzle with olive oil or butter, and serve with the beef ragu on top.

Macronutrient Profile (per serving)

	Grams	Calories	%-Cals
Calories		492	
Fat	32	282	57%
Saturated	9	84	17%
Polyunsaturated	3	24	5%
Monounsaturated	17	148	30%
Carbohydrate	24	86	17%
Dietary Fibre	6		
Protein	31	124	25%

ASPARAGUS AND DRIED MUSHROOMS WITH STEAK

Time in the Kitchen: 25 minutes
Servings: 2

2 steaks

30 g (1¼ oz) dried morels

60 g (2¼ oz) dried porcini

3 tablespoons butter or olive oil

1 large bunch asparagus spears

1 shallot, finely chopped

2–3 garlic cloves, finely chopped

sea salt to taste

Drying mushrooms intensifies the earthy flavour, so this dish is for those who really love their fungi. Dried morel mushrooms can be quite expensive, so if they're above your budget, simply substitute in another kind of dried mushroom. In the autumn and winter when asparagus isn't in season, broccoli raab is also delicious in this dish.

Lightly season your steaks and cook using your favourite method.

As the steaks cook, place the mushrooms in a bowl with just enough hot water to cover them. Cover the bowl with clingfilm and set aside for at least 10 minutes. Next, drain mushrooms but reserve 125 ml (4 fl oz) of the liquid on the side.

Remove the tough bottom ends of the asparagus spears by snapping them off. Cut the spears diagonally into 2.5-cm (1-in) pieces.

In a frying pan over a medium heat, warm butter or olive oil (or a combination of the two) then add shallot, garlic and asparagus. Sauté for 3–5 minutes, stirring so the garlic doesn't burn. Add the mushrooms and a pinch of salt and sauté one minute more.

Add the 125 ml (4 fl oz) of reserved mushroom broth and turn the heat up to high, bringing the liquid to a rapid simmer for 5–8 minutes.

Season with sea salt and serve asparagus and mushrooms on the side of your steak.

Macronutrient Profile (per serving)

	Grams	Calories	%-Cals
Calories		841	
Fat	55	494	59%
Saturated	16	145	17%
Polyunsaturated	4	35	4%
Monounsaturated	29	258	31%
Carbohydrate	18	63	8%
Dietary Fibre	7		
Protein	70	285	34%

SKIRT STEAK AND TURNIP RISOTTO

Time in the Kitchen: 25 minutes
Servings: 4

475 ml (16 fl oz) chicken stock

3–4 large turnips

2 tablespoons unsalted butter

450 g (1 lb) skirt steak

1 shallot

60 ml (2 fl oz) oil

12 g (⅓ oz) fresh herbs to garnish, finely chopped (or more to taste)

This Primal version of risotto cooks a lot faster than the traditional rice version, and eliminates a lot of carbs by using grated turnip instead. The flavour is mild with a bit of earthiness and the texture is soft and comforting – perfect for a chilly winter night.

In a small pot, bring the chicken stock to the boil. Peel turnips and grate in a food processor.

In a large pot, melt the butter at a medium-high heat. Add the turnips and stir. Add the chicken stock and keep at a rapid boil, stirring occasionally, for 10–12 minutes.

While the turnips are cooking, slice the skirt steak into thin strips and lightly season with salt and pepper. Heat a few tablespoons of oil in a frying pan over a high heat. When the pan is very hot, add the steak and cook until it reaches desired doneness.

Peel the shallot and slice very thinly. Heat 60 ml (2 fl oz) of oil; you'll know it's hot enough if you drop a little shallot in and it begins to sizzle immediately. Add the remaining shallot and brown for about one minute until it's nice and crispy, but not burnt.

Stir steak and fresh herbs in with the turnip. Garnish with crispy shallot.

For additional creaminess, stir butter, whole cream or grated Parmesan cheese into the risotto before serving.

Macronutrient Profile (per serving)

	Grams	Calories	%-Cals
Calories		479	
Fat	34	301	63%
Saturated	11	98	21%
Polyunsaturated	2	21	4%
Monounsaturated	19	165	34%
Carbohydrate	10	37	8%
Dietary Fibre	3		
Protein	33	141	29%

Quick & Easy Tip:

If you end up with extra grated turnip, no problem! Use it to make **Turnip Hash Browns** (page 42) for breakfast.

FISH TACOS WITH CITRUS DRESSING

Time in the Kitchen: 20 minutes
Servings: 4

900 g (2 lb) fish (Cod and Halibut work well)

2 tablespoons lemon pepper seasoning

olive oil for drizzling

1 white or red onion, thinly sliced

lettuce leaves to wrap fish in, and/or thinly sliced cabbage to serve on the side

sliced avocados to garnish (optional)

Dressing:

225 g (8 oz) mayonnaise

3 large or 4 small limes (for the zest and juice)

2 garlic cloves, finely chopped

This simple and tasty recipe for fish tacos is one my daughter's favourites, and has become a favourite meal of mine as well. The creamy citrus dressing is what really makes the dish. In fact, the dressing is so good that you may want to save some to top a salad later in the week.

Season the fish with lemon pepper and drizzle olive oil on top. The fish can either be pan-fried, grilled or barbecued, and should only take about 4 minutes per side to cook.

While the fish is cooking, use a grater to remove the green peel from the limes and make zest. Cut the limes open and squeeze out the juice. Stir together the mayonnaise, garlic and lime zest, Slowly add the lime juice until the flavour and consistency of the dressing are to your taste.

Drizzle the dressing over the fish, lettuce leaves and/ or cabbage and garnish with sliced onion.

Macronutrient Profile (per serving)

	Grams	Calories	%-Cals
Calories		701	
Fat	48	429	61%
Saturated	7	65	9%
Polyunsaturated	25	218	31%
Monounsaturated	14	120	17%
Carbohydrate	13	41	6%
Dietary Fibre	3		
Protein	54	228	33%

LAMB BURGERS WITH PISTACHIO PESTO

Time in the Kitchen: 30 minutes
Servings: 4

675 g (1½ lb) lamb mince

1 teaspoon cumin

¼ teaspoon cinnamon

¼ teaspoon allspice

½ teaspoon salt

¼ teaspoon black pepper

15 g (½ oz) mint leaves, finely chopped

15 g (½ oz) parsley, chopped

Pesto Ingredients:

1 garlic clove

150 g (5 oz) unsalted shelled pistachios

125 ml (4 fl oz) olive oil

1 teaspoon lemon juice, or more to taste

15 g (½ oz) loosely packed mint leaves

a pinch of sea salt

Richer than your average burger, this dish is a nice change from the usual beef burger with mustard and ketchup. The pistachio pesto has such a thick texture that you won't even miss the cheese.

Mix together the lamb mince with the remaining burger ingredients. Form four patties and pan-fry, grill or barbecue them, about 4–6 minutes per side.

While the burgers are cooking, blend together pesto ingredients in a food processor.

Serve burgers with pesto drizzled on top.

Macronutrient Profile (per serving)

	Grams	Calories	%-Cals
Calories		916	
Fat	75	664	72%
Saturated	19	172	19%
Polyunsaturated	10	85	9%
Monounsaturated	42	367	40%
Carbohydrate	12	47	5%
Dietary Fibre	6		
Protein	50	205	22%

Quick & Easy Tip:

If you're making a large batch of pesto to eat over the course of a week, keep the colour of the pesto brighter and greener by blanching the basil leaves before making the pesto.

ARTICHOKE AND GREEN OLIVE DIP

Time in the Kitchen: 10 minutes
Servings: 475 ml (16 fl oz) *(macronutrient profile based on serving size of 2½ tablespoons)*

175 g (6 oz) stoned green olives

2   425 g (15 oz) cans/jars of artichoke hearts, drained

1   tablespoon capers, drained

1   garlic clove

1   tablespoon fresh parsley

⅛–¼ teaspoon chilli flakes

salt to taste

Served with a vegetable platter or used as a topping for fish, the zippy flavours in this dip are hard to resist. In addition to tasting great together, the combination of artichokes and olives also brings fibre, monounsaturated fat, vitamin E, calcium, iron and other essential minerals.

Mix all ingredients in a food processor, pulsing until combined but still a little chunky. Add salt to taste.

To give the dip richer flavour, stir in 60–125 ml (2–4 fl oz) olive oil before serving.

Macronutrient Profile (per serving)

	Grams	Calories	%-Cals
Calories		46	
Fat	3	24	52%
Saturated	0	4	8%
Polyunsaturated	0	4	8%
Monounsaturated	2	15	33%
Carbohydrate	5	18	39%
Dietary Fibre	3		
Protein	2	4	8%

CRAB DIP WITH CUCUMBER

Time in the Kitchen: 10 minutes
Servings: 225 ml (8 fl oz) *(macronutrient profile based on serving size of 2½ tablespoons)*

1   teaspoon tomato purée
60 g (2¼ oz) mayonnaise
1   tablespoon chopped chives
1   teaspoon lemon juice
1   teaspoon horseradish
    dash of Tabasco or other hot sauce
225 g (8 oz) crab meat
1   large cucumber, sliced into rounds

This crab dip isn't anything fancy, but it sure tastes great piled on a crisp slice of cucumber. Put a bowl out at parties and watch it disappear. Lump crab meat, which comes from the body of the crab, has the cleanest, freshest flavour but it's also more expensive. Claw meat has a stronger flavour, but it's less expensive and will work just as well in this dip.

Whisk together tomato purée, mayonnaise, chives, lemon juice, horseradish and hot sauce.

Stir in the crab. Serve with slices of cucumber.

Macronutrient Profile (per serving)

	Grams	Calories	%-Cals
Calories		109	
Fat	8	70	64%
Saturated	1	11	10%
Polyunsaturated	4	37	34%
Monounsaturated	2	17	16%
Carbohydrate	1	5	5%
Dietary Fibre	0		
Protein	8	34	31%

Quick & Easy Tip:

Tomato purée is a condensed form of tomato sauce and has a much stronger flavour. For this reason, recipes typically only call for a very small amount. So what can you do with what's left? Scoop tablespoons of tomato purée onto a sheet of parchment paper and freeze for an hour. Scrape the frozen tomato purée into balls, place them in a freezer bag, then simply take one out, defrost, and add to recipes as needed.

BACON AND MUSHROOM DIP

Time in the Kitchen: 15 minutes
Servings: 1 cup *(macronutrient profile based on serving size of 2½ tablespoons)*

6 rashers of bacon

140 g (4½ oz) sliced chestnut or button mushrooms

3 spring onions

125 g (4 oz) mayonnaise

juice of half a lemon, or more to taste

This creamy dip is so good you might want to eat it with a spoon, but try dipping some chopped veggies into it instead. If you serve this dip at a party, make sure to try some before you put it out as it's sure to disappear quickly!

Fry the bacon and sauté mushrooms in the same pan until browned. Add extra oil to sauté the mushrooms if necessary.

Blend the bacon and mushrooms in a food processor with remaining ingredients.

Macronutrient Profile (per serving)

	Grams	Calories	%-Cals
Calories		193	
Fat	18	159	83%
Saturated	3	30	15%
Polyunsaturated	8	73	38%
Monounsaturated	5	45	24%
Carbohydrate	4	16	8%
Dietary Fibre	1		
Protein	4	17	9%

CINNAMON WALNUT CRACKERS

Time in the Kitchen: 30 minutes
Servings: 12 crackers *(macronutrient profile based on serving size of 2 crackers)*

200 g (7 oz) walnuts
1 teaspoon bicarbonate of soda
¼ teaspoon salt
3 teaspoons cinnamon
2 tablespoons melted butter
1 tablespoon honey
1 tablespoon water

Slightly sweet and incredibly rich, these crackers can be treated as a sweet or savoury treat. Walnuts are a healthy source of fat, antioxidants and protein. Serve the crackers with dip or simply eat them alone as an afternoon snack with coffee or tea. The crackers are best eaten the day they are made but will keep in an airtight container.

Preheat oven to 190°C/375°F/Gas Mark 5.

In a food processor or blender, pulse walnuts, bicarbonate of soda, salt and cinnamon until powdery, about 40 seconds. Either in the blender/processor or in a separate bowl, add butter, honey and water and mix until a smooth paste forms.

Cover a baking tray with parchment paper. Using a rubber spatula, gently smear the batter, which will be sticky and wet, onto the parchment paper. Try to form a rectangle that is roughly 28x20 cm (11x8 in).

Bake 12–15 minutes until firm and browned, but not burnt.

Remove from oven and leave to cool completely before using a knife to cut into 12 crackers.

Macronutrient Profile (per serving)

	Grams	Calories	%-Cals
Calories		309	
Fat	30	252	82%
Saturated	5	42	14%
Polyunsaturated	19	159	51%
Monounsaturated	5	39	13%
Carbohydrate	9	36	11%
Dietary Fibre	3		
Protein	6	22	7%

CHOCOLATE COCONUT BARK

Time in the Kitchen: 25 minutes
Servings: 12 squares *(macronutrient profile based on serving size of 1 square)*

55 g (2 oz) dark chocolate
225 ml (8 fl oz) coconut oil
a handful of coconut flakes
a handful of flaked almonds
½ teaspoon sea salt

A small square of this frozen dessert will both satisfy a sweet tooth and give you a good dose of healthy fat from coconut oil. I love to experiment with coconut bark (using various nuts or adding berries) but this version just might be my favourite. Make sure to use high-quality chocolate with 60% cacao or more, and don't forget the sprinkle of sea salt on top to really make the flavour sing.

Fill a pot with a few inches of water, then balance a smaller pot on top so it hovers just above the water (this is called a "bain marie"). Bring the water to a simmer. Break the chocolate into small pieces and melt it in the top pot.

Take the melted chocolate off the heat and stir in coconut oil until it melts. Add coconut and almonds.

Pour batter into a 20x20-cm (8x8-in) baking dish lined with parchment paper. Sprinkle sea salt on top.

Put in the freezer for 15 minutes until solid, then cut into squares. Store the Chocolate Coconut Bark in the freezer.

Macronutrient Profile *(per serving)*

	Grams	Calories	%-Cals
Calories		229	
Fat	24	203	89%
Saturated	18	152	67%
Polyunsaturated	1	9	4%
Monounsaturated	4	30	13%
Carbohydrate	6	21	9%
Dietary Fibre	1		
Protein	2	5	2%

SPICED NUTS

Time in the Kitchen: 20 minutes
Servings: 300 g (11 oz) *(macronutrient profile based on serving size of 55 g/2 oz)*

150 g (5 oz) hazelnuts
100 g (3½ oz) walnuts
1 tablespoon butter
¼ teaspoon salt
¼ teaspoon cinnamon
¼ teaspoon nutmeg
  zest of 1 orange

Most spiced nuts are coated with sugar, but you really don't need sugar to satisfy a sweet craving when you eat these spiced nuts. Lightly roasted nuts have a sweetness all of their own and hints of orange zest, cinnamon and nutmeg add to the impression of sweetness.

Preheat oven to 190°C/375°F/Gas Mark 5.

Place the nuts in a single layer on a rimmed baking sheet. Roast for 10 minutes.

When the nuts are done, melt butter in a pan over a medium heat. When it begins to brown, add salt, cinnamon, nutmeg and orange zest. Add nuts to the pan and mix well.

Serve immediately or store in an airtight container for up to a week.

Macronutrient Profile (per serving)

	Grams	Calories	%-Cals
Calories		268	
Fat	27	223	83%
Saturated	3	28	10%
Polyunsaturated	10	81	30%
Monounsaturated	12	103	38%
Carbohydrate	6	25	9%
Dietary Fibre	3		
Protein	6	21	8%

SPANISH ALMONDS AND OLIVES

Time in the Kitchen: 10 minutes
Servings: 2–4 *(macronutrient profile based on 4 servings)*

zest of 1 lemon

2 tablespoons sherry vinegar

60 ml (2 fl oz) olive oil

2 tablespoons fresh thyme

¼ teaspoon chilli flakes

175 g (6 oz) Spanish olives, such as gordal, manzanilla and arbequina

75 g (2¾ oz) almonds

You'll be amazed by how this zesty, slightly spicy marinade transforms simple olives and almonds into an amazing appetizer or snack. The olives and almonds are ready to eat immediately, but will continue to soak up flavour if refrigerated over the course of a week. If you can't find Spanish olives, any simple blend of olives will benefit from this flavourful marinade.

Whisk together lemon zest, vinegar, olive oil, thyme and chilli flakes. Pour over olives and almonds.

Macronutrient Profile (per serving)

	Grams	Calories	%-Cals
Calories		263	
Fat	26	226	86%
Saturated	3	27	10%
Polyunsaturated	4	34	13%
Monounsaturated	18	158	60%
Carbohydrate	6	22	8%
Dietary Fibre	3		
Protein	4	14	5%

CUCUMBERS AND MINT

Time in the Kitchen: 15 minutes
Servings: 3

9   small Persian or ordinary
    small cucumbers

2   tablespoons olive oil

25 g (1 oz) fresh mint, finely
    chopped

    sea salt to taste

Cooking cucumbers, rather than eating them raw, subtly changes the flavour without losing the crisp, refreshing qualities that make cucumbers so popular. Grilling is the fastest method, but you can try sautéing or barbecuing cukes, too. Any type of cucumber can be used in this recipe, but small Persian cucumbers consistently have good flavour and a crunchy texture.

Preheat grill to a low heat.

Cut cucumbers in half lengthways, then in half again.

Drizzle cucumbers with olive oil and put under the grill for five minutes. The cucumbers will soften but still have some crispness.

Remove from oven and sprinkle with mint. Add sea salt to taste.

Macronutrient Profile (per serving)

	Grams	Calories	%-Cals
Calories		153	
Fat	10	89	57%
Saturated	1	12	8%
Polyunsaturated	1	10	6%
Monounsaturated	7	58	38%
Carbohydrate	13	52	34%
Dietary Fibre	6		
Protein	4	14	9%

ROASTED RADISHES

Time in the Kitchen: 30 minutes
Servings: 4–6 *(macronutrient profile based on 6 servings)*

3 bunches of radishes
60 ml (2 fl oz) olive oil
¼ teaspoon pepper
¼ teaspoon salt
juice of 1 lemon

Roasting radishes mellows the spicy flavour and turns them into slightly crunchy, delectable morsels. Lemon and salt are the easiest ways to season roasted radishes, but adding chopped garlic, parsley and/or anchovy will up the flavour. Serve the radishes before dinner with cocktail sticks or as a side dish.

Preheat oven to 240°C/475°F/Gas Mark 9.

Cut leaves and stems off radishes. Slice smaller radishes into halves and larger ones into thirds.

Place in a baking dish and cover with olive oil, salt and pepper. Bake 15–20 minutes, stirring once or twice. Finish with lemon juice to taste and a sprinkle of sea salt if needed.

Macronutrient Profile (per serving)

	Grams	Calories	%-Cals
Calories		162	
Fat	15	124	77%
Saturated	3	26	16%
Polyunsaturated	3	29	18%
Monounsaturated	8	63	39%
Carbohydrate	6	25	15%
Dietary Fibre	3		
Protein	4	13	8%

TURNIP AND SWEDE FRIES

Time in the Kitchen: 30 minutes
Servings: 4

2 peeled swedes

2 peeled turnips

60 ml (2 fl oz) olive oil

1 teaspoon dried finely chopped garlic, or 1 tablespoon fresh garlic, finely chopped

1 teaspoon salt

Turnips and swedes vary greatly in size, so you might need to buy more than two if they are small. It's better to err on the side of buying more rather than less, as these fries will get eaten quickly! After you make the fries once, start experimenting with flavours. Adding fresh herbs or curry powder are two ways to change things up.

Preheat oven to 230°C/450°F/Gas Mark 8.

Cut turnips and swedes into spears about 1-cm (½-in) wide and drizzle olive oil on top. Microwave for 8 minutes.

Transfer fries to a baking dish and sprinkle with garlic and salt. Bake for 15–18 minutes, stirring once or twice so they don't burn. Add more oil as they bake if needed.

Serve immediately, as the fries tend to get soggy if they sit around too long.

Macronutrient Profile (per serving)

	Grams	Calories	%-Cals
Calories		205	
Fat	14	123	60%
Saturated	2	17	8%
Polyunsaturated	2	14	7%
Monounsaturated	10	88	43%
Carbohydrate	19	74	36%
Dietary Fibre	4		
Protein	3	8	4%

Quick & Easy Tip:

Turnips and swedes are sometimes hard to tell apart. Typically, although not always, turnips have a purple tinge to the skin and white flesh. Swedes usually have a yellow tinge to the flesh.

CHICORY WITH HONEY AND WALNUTS

Time in the Kitchen: 25 minutes
Servings: 4

4–6 heads chicory
4 tablespoons butter
100 g (3½ oz) walnuts
1 tablespoon honey
1 tablespoon fresh thyme
sea salt to taste

This dish is easiest to serve as a first course salad, as the cooked chicory is too soft to pass as finger food. The pleasant bitterness in chicory is contrasted perfectly with the sweet honey and walnuts. Make sure to finish the dish with a sprinkle of sea salt, as it really brings out the flavour.

NOTE: If you use 6 chicory heads, you'll need at least a 30-cm (12-in) frying pan. 4 chicory heads will fit in a slightly smaller frying pan.

Take the first layer of leaves off the chicory and discard. Cut the chicory lengthways into quarters, removing as much of the bitter inner core as possible (without releasing the leaves).

In a large pan, melt 2 tablespoons of butter over a medium heat and lay chicory in one even layer. Sprinkle walnuts on top. Cover the pan with a lid and cook for five minutes.

While the chicory is cooking, melt the remaining butter with the honey and thyme, either in the microwave or on the hob.

Turn the chicory over and drizzle the butter and honey mixture on top. Cover again for another five minutes. Remove lid and sauté 3–5 minutes more so the chicory becomes slightly browned and caramelized.

Sprinkle with sea salt and serve.

Macronutrient Profile (per serving)

	Grams	Calories	%-Cals
Calories		446	
Fat	33	278	63%
Saturated	10	83	19%
Polyunsaturated	15	128	29%
Monounsaturated	6	49	11%
Carbohydrate	34	125	28%
Dietary Fibre	26		
Protein	14	40	9%

BARBECUED SARDINES WITH TARRAGON DRESSING

Time in the Kitchen: 20 minutes
Servings: 2

- 65 g (2½ oz) pine nuts
- 2 tablespoons butter
- 1 shallot, finely chopped
- 1 tablespoon lemon zest
  juice of 1 lemon (plus more lemons to garnish)
- 1 tablespoon capers
- 1 teaspoon tarragon, finely chopped, or more to taste
- 1 bunch watercress, lamb's lettuce or other greens
- 12 fresh sardines, gutted and scaled

Most of us are used to eating sardines out of a can for a healthy dose of omega-3 fat, but never think about barbecuing fresh sardines. The fresh sardines sold at most fish counters are 2–3 times bigger than the canned varieties, but the flavour is very similar. A simple tarragon dressing adds a pleasantly aromatic topping that subdues any 'fishiness'.

NOTE: When canned, it's customary to eat the sardine, bones and all. Fresh sardine bones shouldn't be eaten; your fishmonger can fillet the fish for you beforehand. Whether or not you want the head removed is personal preference. If you want to fillet the fish yourself at home, follow these steps:

1. Cut open the belly from head to tail and spread open the fillet.
2. Discard the innards.
3. Grasp the spine and gently work the bones away from the flesh.
4. Snip or cut the spine off where it meats the tail.

Preheat your barbecue to high heat.

In a pan over a medium heat, lightly toast the pine nuts. Watch out – pine nuts burn quickly! Remove the nuts from heat and put in a bowl.

In the same pan, melt the butter and sauté the shallot until softened. Add the shallot to the pine nuts. Mix in lemon zest, lemon juice, capers and tarragon. Toss half of the dressing with the greens.

Brush the sardines with olive oil or butter and lightly salt and pepper. Barbecue sardines until lightly charred, about 2 minutes on each side.

Lay sardines on greens. Top with remaining dressing and serve with lemon wedges.

Macronutrient Profile (per serving)

	Grams	Calories	%-Cals
Calories		410	
Fat	38	328	80%
Saturated	9	83	20%
Polyunsaturated	14	115	28%
Monounsaturated	11	90	22%
Carbohydrate	8	30	7%
Dietary Fibre	2		
Protein	14	52	13%

SCALLOPS WITH ALMONDS AND BACON

Time in the Kitchen: 20 minutes
Servings: 3

4 rashers of bacon
75 g (2¾ oz) almonds
1 large handful parsley
1 tablespoon olive oil
1 tablespoon butter
450 g (1 lb) scallops

Mild, buttery scallops and salty, meaty bacon are a perfect example of why sparks fly when opposites attract. If you've had bacon-wrapped scallops before, this starter is similar but takes the flavour to the next level. Almonds add a satisfying crunch and a hefty dose of manganese, potassium, copper, vitamin E and heart healthy monounsaturated fats.

Cook the bacon until crispy, then cool slightly and crumble into a food processor with almonds and parsley. Pulse until almonds are in small pieces.

Heat the oil and butter in a large frying pan over a medium-high heat until the butter foam subsides (if you prefer, you can cook the scallops in the leftover bacon grease, rather than the butter and olive oil).

Add the scallops to the frying pan. Turn the heat to high and cook for about 2 minutes or until scallops are brown on one side, then turn and brown the other side for another minute or two. This will leave the scallops cooked, but rare in the middle. If you prefer a firmer texture, cook the scallops 1–2 minutes more.

Transfer the scallops to a plate and sprinkle with bacon nut mixture.

Macronutrient Profile (per serving)

	Grams	Calories	%-Cals
Calories		413	
Fat	28	241	58%
Saturated	6	50	12%
Polyunsaturated	5	45	11%
Monounsaturated	15	128	31%
Carbohydrate	10	38	9%
Dietary Fibre	3		
Protein	33	134	32%

SQUID WITH TOMATO AND BASIL

Time in the Kitchen: 25 minutes
Servings: 4

2 large tomatoes, cut into slices or wedges

55 g (2 oz) fresh basil, roughly chopped

4 tablespoons olive oil

450 g (1 lb) cleaned squid, bodies and tentacles

3 garlic cloves, finely chopped

1 teaspoon salt

This salad is the perfect summer starter, when tomatoes are ripe and juicy and the intense aroma of basil perfumes the whole dish. Squid is so mild in flavour that it eagerly picks up the flavour of the garlic and olive oil marinade even though it only soaks in it for a few minutes.

Heat barbecue to high or preheat grill to high.

Combine tomatoes and basil on a platter. Drizzle with 2 tablespoons of olive oil.

Rinse squid and pat dry. Toss with garlic, salt, and remaining 2 tablespoons of olive oil.

If barbecuing, thread squid on skewers, separating bodies and tentacles on different skewers.* If cooking under the grill, simply put squid in a pan. Cook squid until it firms up, about 5–7 minutes.

Toss squid with tomatoes and basil. Add additional salt and olive oil to taste.

* *If using wooden skewers, soak them in water before using.*

Macronutrient Profile (per serving)

	Grams	Calories	%-Cals
Calories		273	
Fat	16	140	51%
Saturated	2	21	8%
Polyunsaturated	2	21	8%
Monounsaturated	10	89	33%
Carbohydrate	11	40	15%
Dietary Fibre	3		
Protein	23	92	34%

Quick & Easy Tip:

A tomato knife, which is simply a small, serrated knife, can be bought for around £6 and is worth every penny. The knife easily slices through the skin of a tomato, making dicing or slicing a tomato quick work.

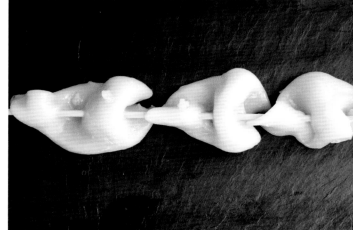

KOREAN-STYLE BLACKBERRY RIBS

Time in the Kitchen: 25 minutes
Servings: 4

125 ml (4 fl oz) sesame oil

150 g (5 oz) blackberries, frozen (defrosted) or fresh

60 ml (2 fl oz) tamari

25 g (1 oz) ginger slices

1 garlic clove

2 tablespoons rice wine vinegar

900 g (2 lb) beef short ribs

1 bunch spring onions

The addictive finger-licking flavour of Korean beef short ribs usually comes from adding lots of sugar (or corn syrup) to the marinade. Ditch the sugar and use berries instead to infuse a sweet flavour that's also rich with antioxidants.

These ribs can be cooked on the barbecue or under a grill. If using a barbecue, bring it up to a high heat while you make the marinade. The grill should also be used on a high heat.

Combine 60 ml (2 fl oz) of the sesame oil, plus the next five ingredients in the blender until the marinade has a smoothie-like consistency.

Place the ribs in a container and pour the marinade on top. Flip the ribs around so they are well-covered with the marinade.

In a separate container, coat the spring onions with the remaining 60 ml (2 fl oz) of sesame oil.

Place the ribs and spring onions on the barbecue or under the grill. Cook the ribs for 4–6 minutes on each side, until the outside is a bit crispy and caramelized. The spring onions will wilt and brown, but should be taken away from heat before they burn.

Macronutrient Profile (per serving)

	Grams	Calories	%-Cals
Calories		1345	
Fat	122	1099	82%
Saturated	44	397	30%
Polyunsaturated	15	133	10%
Monounsaturated	54	481	36%
Carbohydrate	8	28	2%
Dietary Fibre	3		
Protein	51	217	16%

SAVOURY CREPES

Time in the Kitchen: 20 minutes
Servings: 4 crêpes *(macronutrient profile
based on serving size of 1 crêpe)*

125 ml (4 fl oz) coconut milk*

2 tablespoons melted butter

4 tablespoons coconut flour

8 egg whites**

* You can adjust the thickness
and texture of the crêpe by
adding a little more coconut
milk to the batter if you like.

** The yolks can be saved for
another meal, or scrambled
with butter and used as a
filling for the crêpes.

Filling suggestions:

- **Smoked salmon**
- **Prosciutto or Parma Ham**
- **Seasoned pork mince. Try
  using the recipe for** *Pork and
  Shiitake Lettuce Cups* **(page
  84).**
- **Fresh herbs**
- **Sautéed mushrooms**
- **Sautéed prawns (Try adding
  spring onions and tamari to
  the crêpe batter.)**

I'll let you in on a secret; these crêpes are delicious served with cinnamon, butter and fresh berries, too, but for a starter I prefer savoury fillings. The options for fillings are endless. A few great ones to try are listed in the ingredients panel.

In a large bowl, slowly pour the coconut milk and butter over the coconut flour, whisking and mashing with a fork so a smooth paste forms.

Briskly whisk the egg whites so they get nice and frothy. Pour the egg whites in with the coconut paste in four additions, whisking well with a fork or whisk between each addition. Adding the egg whites slowly ensures that the batter will be smooth; otherwise, coconut flour can clump together and be lumpy.

Add a tablespoon of oil or butter to a 10-inch frying pan over a medium heat. Pour just enough batter in the pan to coat the base (you should have enough batter to make 4 crêpes). Quickly swirl the pan around so the batter spreads evenly.

If necessary, after one minute you can gently loosen the edges of the crêpe by sliding a rubber spatula underneath the crêpe to prevent sticking.

After three minutes, flip the crêpe with a large, flat pancake turner or a spatula. If you are adding a filling that you want to warm up, you can add it now across the middle of the crêpe and put a lid on the frying pan. If you are not adding a filling, it is not necessary to put a lid on the pan.

Either way, cook for 2 more minutes, then fold the crêpe and slide it out of the pan.

Macronutrient Profile (per serving)

	Grams	Calories	%-Cals
Calories		248	
Fat	22	188	76%
Saturated	18	153	62%
Polyunsaturated	0	4	1%
Monounsaturated	2	19	8%
Carbohydrate	6	22	9%
Dietary Fibre	3		
Protein	9	37	15%

BACON-WRAPPED CHICKEN LIVERS

Time in the Kitchen: 25 minutes
Servings: 4

450 g (1 lb) chicken livers
350 g (12 oz) packet of bacon

Just about everything tastes better with bacon wrapped around it, and liver is no exception. Bacon-wrapped chicken livers are packed with protein and an abundance of vitamin A and several B vitamins, folic acid, iron, copper and CoQ10, which is important for cardio-vascular function.

Cut the chicken livers so they are in similar shapes and sizes.

In a pan over a medium heat, cook livers in a little oil for two minutes on each side.

Remove livers from the pan and leave to cool slightly. Wrap one piece of bacon tightly around each liver so that the liver is almost entirely covered by bacon.

Return bacon-wrapped livers to the pan and continue to cook over a medium heat for about 3 minutes on each side, until bacon is nicely browned and the liver is firm, but still slightly pink in the middle.

Macronutrient Profile (per serving)

	Grams	Calories	%-Cals
Calories		648	
Fat	43	387	60%
Saturated	14	126	20%
Polyunsaturated	5	48	7%
Monounsaturated	17	157	24%
Carbohydrate	2	9	1%
Dietary Fibre	0		
Protein	59	252	39%

The Primal Blueprint Quick & Easy Cookbook   **175**

CHICKEN WITH ALMOND COCONUT DIPPING SAUCE

Time in the Kitchen: 20 minutes
Servings: 3

675 g (1½ lb) chicken breast, cut into thin strips

Chicken Seasoning:

3   tablespoons tamari

2   teaspoons coriander

1   teaspoon cumin

1   tablespoon sesame oil

Dipping Sauce:

125 g (4 oz) almond butter

60 ml (2 fl oz) coconut milk

60 ml (2 fl oz) water

1   garlic clove

2   teaspoons ginger, finely chopped

1   teaspoon tamari

3   teaspoons sesame oil

1½ tablespoons fish sauce

This recipe is similar to chicken satay, but uses almond sauce instead of peanut sauce for dipping. It's an easy starter and also a popular afternoon snack for kids.

Turn grill or a barbecue to high heat.

Season the chicken with tamari, sesame oil, coriander and cumin. Grill or barbecue for 10 minutes, until chicken is cooked through.

Put all the ingredients for the dipping sauce into a food processor (the sauce can also be whisked together by hand). Process or whisk until smooth.

Serve the dipping sauce with the chicken. Garnish with chopped spring onions if desired.

Macronutrient Profile (per serving)

	Grams	Calories	%-Cals
Calories		760	
Fat	45	383	50%
Saturated	10	85	11%
Polyunsaturated	10	89	12%
Monounsaturated	21	182	24%
Carbohydrate	12	47	6%
Dietary Fibre	3		
Protein	79	329	43%

PIGS IN
A BLANKET

Time in the Kitchen: 20 minutes
Servings: 4

6–8 pork sausages
1 head of cabbage
   mustard for dipping
   cocktail sticks

Set out a plate and watch these little piggies wrapped in cabbage blankets disappear! They are easiest to eat if cut into bite-sized pieces and speared with a cocktail stick.

Barbecue or grill sausages for 8–10 minutes, or until done.

Peel the leaves off the head of cabbage. Cut out the bottom half of the middle stem from each leaf, as this part tends to be tough and chewy. Microwave the leaves for 3–5 minutes, or until soft. If the cabbage leaves are too dry for your liking, drizzle with a little melted butter.

Set a sausage on the far end of a cabbage leaf and roll the leaf up. Secure the leaf around the sausage with several cocktail sticks. If the sausages are short, you can roll the leaf twice, then fold the sides in and continue rolling.

Cut cabbage-wrapped sausages into bite-sized pieces and serve with mustard for dipping.

Macronutrient Profile (per serving)

	Grams	Calories	%-Cals
Calories		191	
Fat	13	117	61%
Saturated	3	31	16%
Polyunsaturated	3	24	12%
Monounsaturated	6	53	28%
Carbohydrate	12	45	23%
Dietary Fibre	4		
Protein	8	30	15%

LAMB MEATBALLS

Time in the Kitchen: 25 minutes
Servings: 12 meatballs *(macronutrient profile based on serving size of 3 meatballs)*

450 g (1 lb) lamb mince

1 egg

15 g (½ oz) dill or parsley, chopped

2 garlic cloves, finely chopped

¼ teaspoon cinnamon

¼ teaspoon allspice

½ teaspoon cumin

½ teaspoon paprika

½ teaspoon salt

35 g (1¼ oz) pine nuts

The aromatic spices and pine nuts add a slight sweetness to these rich lamb meatballs. Make a batch to keep in your fridge for snacks on the go, or serve these as a side with any type of vegetable to turn the meatballs into a full meal.

Mix together all ingredients.

Form lamb mince into 12 meatballs.

Warm a tablespoon of oil in a frying pan over a medium-high heat. Add meatballs and brown for 2 minutes, then turn and brown the other side for 2 minutes. Turn the heat down to medium and put a lid on the pan. Cook for 10–12 more minutes, until meatballs are no longer pink in the middle.

Macronutrient Profile (per serving)

	Grams	Calories	%-Cals
Calories		401	
Fat	30	263	66%
Saturated	10	90	22%
Polyunsaturated	5	41	10%
Monounsaturated	12	104	26%
Carbohydrate	2	8	2%
Dietary Fibre	1		
Protein	31	130	32%

COCONUT CURRY MEATBALLS

Time in the Kitchen: 30 minutes
Servings: 24 meatballs *(macronutrient profile based on serving size of 4 meatballs)*

675 g (1½ lb) boneless skinless chicken

1 carrot, grated

2 garlic cloves

25 g (1 oz) coconut flakes

1 egg

2 teaspoons curry powder

½ teaspoon salt

a handful of coriander (or parsley)

These meatballs are so good you might want to promote them from starter to main course. You can buy pre-minced meat if you like, but it takes hardly any time to mince it yourself in the food processor. A combination of thigh and breast meat yields a moist meatball that will hold together well.

Put everything in the food processor and pulse until smooth.

Using your hands, form 24 meatballs. The smaller size of these meatballs allows them to cook quickly.

Heat several tablespoons of oil in a large frying pan over a medium-high heat. When the frying pan is hot enough so that a meatball sizzles as soon as it hits the pan, put all the meatballs in.

Cook two minutes then roll the meatballs over and cook five minutes more. Put a lid on the pan and finish cooking for a further 6–8 minutes.

Macronutrient Profile (per serving)

	Grams	Calories	%-Cals
Calories		260	
Fat	11	101	39%
Saturated	4	37	14%
Polyunsaturated	2	19	7%
Monounsaturated	4	32	12%
Carbohydrate	4	16	6%
Dietary Fibre	1		
Protein	34	145	55%

BARBECUED DUCK SKEWERS WITH SPICED BUTTER GLAZE

Time in the Kitchen: 30 minutes
Servings: 4

- 4 tablespoons melted butter
- 1 tablespoon honey
- 1 tablespoon tamari
- ½ teaspoon Chinese five spice powder
- 4 boneless duck breasts with skin on

  sesame seeds to garnish

Duck really isn't any more complicated to cook than other types of meat, especially if you throw it on the barbecue. The thick layer of skin tastes best when a high heat turns it into a crispy, crunchy coating, so don't be afraid of getting the flames going a bit. The meat itself is most tender when left a bit pink.

Heat the barbecue to high.

In a bowl whisk together butter, honey, tamari and Chinese five spice powder. Separate the glaze into two bowls: one for brushing the raw duck and one for dipping after the duck is cooked.

Cut the duck breasts in half lengthways then into 4 pieces. Put on skewers, brush with half of sauce and barbecue. The heat should be high enough to brown and crisp the duck skin, but you may have to move the skewers around to avoid flare-ups. The cooking time will vary depending on how hot your barbecue is, but will likely take around 12 minutes.

Take the duck off the barbecue and drizzle with the reserved butter glaze or serve the glaze on the side. Sprinkle with sesame seeds.

Macronutrient Profile (per serving)

	Grams	Calories	%-Cals
Calories		606	
Fat	38	336	55%
Saturated	14	127	21%
Polyunsaturated	4	39	6%
Monounsaturated	16	144	24%
Carbohydrate	5	17	3%
Dietary Fibre	0		
Protein	59	253	42%

Quick & Easy Tip:

Instead of relying on a thermometer, use this easy chart to gauge how hot your barbecue is: hold your hand 5 inches above the centre of the barbecue. If you can hold it there for only 2 seconds, it is a hot fire; 3 to 4 seconds, it is a medium-hot fire; 5 to 6 seconds, it is a medium fire; 7 seconds or more, it is a medium-low fire.

SALMON ROE AND CUCUMBER ROUNDS

Time in the Kitchen: 10 minutes
Servings: 15–20 pieces *(macronutrient profile based on serving size of 5 pieces)*

55 g (2 oz) salmon roe

1–2 cucumbers, sliced into rounds

1 avocado, cut into small chunks

1 sheet of nori, cut into small squares

A colourful combination of complementary flavours with no actual cooking required. Just assemble the ingredients into a delicious bite-sized starter.

Lay cucumber rounds on serving platter. Set a square of nori on each cucumber slice and top with avocado and salmon roe.

Macronutrient Profile (per serving)

	Grams	Calories	%-Cals
Calories		120	
Fat	9	72	60%
Saturated	1	11	9%
Polyunsaturated	1	11	9%
Monounsaturated	5	44	36%
Carbohydrate	8	30	24%
Dietary Fibre	4		
Protein	6	19	16%

BARBECUED MUSSELS WITH PARSLEY AND SHALLOT

Time in the Kitchen: 15 minutes
Servings: 4

900 g (2 lb) fresh mussels

1 small shallot, finely chopped

1 tablespoon olive oil or melted butter

15 g (½ oz) parsley, finely chopped

This is a great way to cook mussels outdoors. You can serve this dish on a platter with cocktail sticks, or toss the mussels in a bowl as a seafood salad.

Heat the barbecue to medium.

Clean the mussels in cold water and pull the beards off. The beard looks like threads hanging outside of the shell.

The mussels can be put directly on the barbecue, but it's easier to put them in a grill basket or on foil so they don't fall through the grates. Cook the mussels with the barbecue lid on for 6–8 minutes until they open. Discard any shells that haven't opened.

Combine the shallot, olive oil/butter and parsley.

Shuck the mussels out of their shells and toss with the parsley dressing. Serve warm or chilled.

Macronutrient Profile (per serving)

	Grams	Calories	%-Cals
Calories		420	
Fat	13	121	29%
Saturated	2	22	5%
Polyunsaturated	3	28	7%
Monounsaturated	5	43	10%
Carbohydrate	17	71	17%
Dietary Fibre	0		
Protein	54	229	54%

Quick & Easy Tip:

When a recipe calls for chopped herbs and you're in a hurry, use kitchen scissors to cut fresh herbs into pieces instead of finely chopping the herbs with a knife.

SWEET AND SPICY COCONUT SAUCE

Time in the Kitchen: 15 minutes
Servings: About 225 ml (8 fl oz) *(macronutrient profile based on serving size of 2 ½ tablespoons)*

1 teaspoon sesame oil

1 shallot, finely chopped

1 tablespoon rice wine vinegar

1 tablespoon sweet chilli sauce

225 ml (8 fl oz) coconut milk

1 tablespoon fresh mint, finely chopped, or more to taste

Sweet chilli sauce is sold in the World Food section of supermarkets and adds a sweet and spicy flavour to creamy coconut milk. This sauce is delicious drizzled over red meat and can be served as a dipping sauce for the ***Coconut Curry Meatballs*** (page 182).

Heat sesame oil in a pan and sauté shallot until soft.

Stir in vinegar and sauté twenty seconds more, then add hot chilli sauce and coconut milk. Simmer until sauce is slightly thickened, about 10 minutes.

Remove from heat. If desired, shallot can be strained out. Stir in fresh mint.

Macronutrient Profile (per serving)

	Grams	Calories	%-Cals
Calories		101	
Fat	10	87	86%
Saturated	9	72	71%
Polyunsaturated	0	4	4%
Monounsaturated	1	6	6%
Carbohydrate	3	11	11%
Dietary Fibre	1		
Protein	1	4	3%

CREAMY CHIPOTLE SAUCE

Time in the Kitchen: 10 minutes
Servings: 225 ml (8 fl oz) *(macronutrient profile based on serving size of 2 ½ tablespoons)*

225 ml (8 fl oz) mayonnaise or sour cream, or 125 ml (4 fl oz) of each

2 tablespoons lime juice

1 teaspoon of adobo sauce from a can of chipotle chillies in adobo

15 g (½ oz) coriander, finely chopped (optional)

This creamy, spicy sauce straddles the line between a sauce and a dressing. It can be drizzled over practically any type of meat or seafood and also works well as a salad dressing. Try it with the **Barbecued Taco Salad** (page 80).

Chipotle chillies in adobo sauce can be found jarred or canned at some supermarkets and speciality grocery stores and have a unique smoky flavour. They're also smokin' hot – don't say you haven't been warned.

Mix together ingredients. Add more lime juice and chipotle sauce to taste.

Macronutrient Profile (per serving)

	Grams	Calories	%-Cals
Calories		265	
Fat	29	254	97%
Saturated	4	39	15%
Polyunsaturated	16	139	53%
Monounsaturated	7	64	24%
Carbohydrate	2	7	3%
Dietary Fibre	0		
Protein	0	2	1%

CREAMY WALNUT SAUCE

Time in the Kitchen: 15 minutes
Servings: 225 ml (8 fl oz) *(macronutrient profile based on serving size of 2½ tablespoons)*

100 g (3½ oz) walnuts

1 shallot, finely chopped

2 tablespoons butter

350 ml (12 fl oz) double cream or coconut milk

salt to taste

This rich and nutty sauce makes everything from roasted vegetables to chicken more interesting. For a Primal take on Chicken Alfredo, sauté thinly sliced courgette with chicken, then pour the sauce on top.

Sauté walnuts and shallot in butter until walnuts are lightly toasted, about 3 minutes.

Add 1 cup of cream or coconut milk and bring to a gentle simmer for five minutes.

Pour the walnuts and cream in a blender and purée until as smooth as possible. Add salt to taste.

This yields a fairly thick sauce. Add the additional ½ cup of cream or coconut milk to thin out if desired. If you want the sauce to be silky smooth, push the puréed sauce through a fine mesh sieve so the nut solids are separated out.

Macronutrient Profile (per serving)

	Grams	Calories	%-Cals
Calories		244	
Fat	24	204	83%
Saturated	8	69	28%
Polyunsaturated	10	83	34%
Monounsaturated	5	41	17%
Carbohydrate	6	22	9%
Dietary Fibre	1		
Protein	5	19	8%

SILKY LEMON AND EGG SAUCE

Time in the Kitchen: 10 minutes
Servings: 475 ml (16 fl oz) *(macronutrient profile based on serving size of 2 ½ tablespoons)*

2 eggs

juice of 1 lemon (about 3 tablespoons)

475 ml (16 fl oz) chicken stock

2 teaspoons arrowroot

1 tablespoon water

By its looks and ingredients you wouldn't think this traditional Greek sauce, often called 'avgolemono' was anything special, but it adds a surprising amount of flavour when drizzled over pretty much anything (especially cooked chicken, fish and vegetables). The bright, lemony flavour comes through whether this sauce is served hot or cold. If you really like it, you might even consider using it as stock for a creamy soup.

If you can't find arrowroot (check the baking aisle at the supermarket) you can still make this sauce, it will taste great, it just won't be as thick.

Whisk eggs with lemon juice really well for at least 30 seconds until completely combined and frothy.

Combine stock and egg mixture in a saucepan over a medium heat. Stir as it comes to the boil. Continue to boil for several minutes.

Mix together arrowroot and water. Remove the sauce from heat and drizzle in the arrowroot while stirring constantly. Within a few minutes, the sauce will thicken.

Macronutrient Profile (per serving)

	Grams	Calories	%-Cals
Calories		24	
Fat	1	11	47%
Saturated	0	3	14%
Polyunsaturated	0	2	8%
Monounsaturated	1	5	19%
Carbohydrate	1	5	20%
Dietary Fibre	0		
Protein	2	8	33%

SPINACH HORSERADISH SAUCE

Time in the Kitchen: 10 minutes
Servings: 225 ml (8 fl oz) *(macronutrient profile based on serving size of 2 ½ tablespoons)*

155 g (5½ oz) frozen chopped spinach (thawed) or 2 large handfuls of fresh spinach

1 small handful (or about 15 g/½ oz) fresh parsley, roughly chopped

2 tablespoons prepared white horseradish (or more to taste)

125 g (4 oz) mayonnaise

2 tablespoons fresh lemon juice

2 spring onions, roughly chopped

This sauce is thick enough to be a dip, and you'll find that it does go really well with a platter of raw vegetables for dipping. Otherwise, spoon it over fish and its lemony flavour will really shine. It's also delicious served with the **Dill and Caper Salmon Burgers** (page 86).

If using defrosted spinach, squeeze it over a colander to get rid of as much moisture as possible.

Mix all ingredients in the food processor until smooth.

Macronutrient Profile (per serving)

	Grams	Calories	%-Cals
Calories		156	
Fat	15	137	88%
Saturated	3	25	16%
Polyunsaturated	8	70	45%
Monounsaturated	4	34	22%
Carbohydrate	4	13	8%
Dietary Fibre	2		
Protein	2	5	3%

MUSTARD SAUCE

Time in the Kitchen: 10 minutes
Servings: 125 ml (4 fl oz) *(macronutrient profile based on serving size of 2½ tablespoons)*

2 tablespoons unsalted butter

1 small shallot

125 ml (4 fl oz) chicken stock

60 g (2¼ oz) Dijon or German mustard

4 tablespoons coconut milk (or double cream)

1 tablespoon parsley, finely chopped

Mustard, especially when mixed into a creamy sauce, always tastes great with pork, although there is no reason you can't use this sauce with other types of meat as well. The coconut milk adds creaminess to this sauce, but doesn't affect the flavour.

Melt butter over a medium heat and add shallot. Sauté until soft.

Add chicken stock and simmer for five minutes.

Add mustard and coconut milk and simmer for two minutes. Stir in parsley.

Macronutrient Profile *(per serving)*

	Grams	Calories	%-Cals
Calories		134	
Fat	13	114	85%
Saturated	9	77	58%
Polyunsaturated	1	5	4%
Monounsaturated	3	25	18%
Carbohydrate	3	11	8%
Dietary Fibre	1		
Protein	2	9	6%

FENNEL PESTO

Time in the Kitchen: 10 minutes
Servings: 225 ml (8 fl oz) *(macronutrient profile based on serving size of 2½ tablespoons)*

1 fennel bulb

15 g (½ oz) fresh basil, roughly chopped

½ teaspoon lemon zest

1 garlic clove

125 ml (4 fl oz) olive oil

35 g (1¼ oz) pine nuts

salt to taste

Creamy and addictive, this cheese-less pesto will quickly become a favourite. Because this pesto is all about the delicate flavour of fennel, it only has a little bit of basil added. You could, however, add more basil and pine nuts to give it a more traditional pesto flavour. Serve as a dip with vegetables or spoon over cooked chicken and fish.

Cut top stems off the fennel bulb but keep the soft, feathery fronds to add to the pesto.

Cut the fennel bulb in half, peel off the outer layer and cut out the inner core. Roughly chop the fennel bulb and combine in the food processor with the fennel fronds, basil, lemon zest, garlic and olive oil. Blend until smooth.

Add the pine nuts and pulse a few times until just blended. Add salt to taste.

Macronutrient Profile (per serving)

	Grams	Calories	%-Cals
Calories		207	
Fat	22	193	93%
Saturated	3	25	12%
Polyunsaturated	4	34	16%
Monounsaturated	14	125	61%
Carbohydrate	2	10	5%
Dietary Fibre	1		
Protein	1	5	2%

CAULIFLOWER CAPONATA

Time in the Kitchen: 30 minutes
Servings: 475 ml (16 fl oz) *(macronutrient profile based on serving size of 2 ½ tablespoons)*

60 ml (2 fl oz) olive oil
1 cauliflower head, broken into very small florets
1 onion, finely diced
1 shallot, finely chopped
1 garlic clove, finely chopped
45 g (1½ oz) sultanas
60 ml (2 fl oz) balsamic vinegar
1 tablespoon honey
¼ teaspoon chilli flakes
½ teaspoon ground cinnamon
⅛ teaspoon ground nutmeg
1 teaspoon cocoa powder
35 g (1¼ oz) toasted pine nuts
salt to taste

Caponata is a Sicilian dish that is traditionally made with aubergine. Every once in while it's good to challenge tradition, and I've done so by using cauliflower instead. This mild vegetable is the perfect backdrop for the bold sweet, savoury and sour flavours that have made caponata such a treasured regional dish. As a sauce, this caponata is especially good spooned over pork.

Add the olive oil to a deep pan over a medium-high heat. When hot, add cauliflower and sauté for several minutes to brown cauliflower slightly.

Add onion and shallot, sauté one minute, then add all the remaining ingredients except pine nuts.

Turn heat to medium-low and simmer with a lid for 10–15 minutes, stirring once or twice. The cauliflower should be soft, but not mushy.

Turn off heat and add pine nuts. Salt to taste.

Macronutrient Profile (per serving)

	Grams	Calories	%-Cals
Calories		90	
Fat	7	57	64%
Saturated	1	7	8%
Polyunsaturated	1	13	14%
Monounsaturated	4	34	38%
Carbohydrate	8	29	32%
Dietary Fibre	1		
Protein	1	3	4%

WALNUT BLUEBERRY RELISH

Time in the Kitchen: 15 minutes
Servings: 225 ml (8 fl oz) *(macronutrient profile based on serving size of 2½ tablespoons)*

100 g (3½ oz) walnuts

90 ml (3 fl oz) balsamic vinegar

75 g (2¾ oz) dried blueberries (with no sugar added)

½ of a small red onion, thinly sliced

1–2 garlic cloves, finely chopped

Simultaneously sweet, savoury and tart, this relish will remind you of crystallized walnuts, but with many more layers of flavour. It's delicious served with pork or simply spooned over a salad.

Preheat oven to 160°C/325°F/Gas Mark 3.

Toast the walnuts in the oven for 10 minutes.

While the walnuts are toasting, combine balsamic vinegar, dried blueberries, red onion, and garlic in a pan over a medium-high heat. Bring to the boil, then turn the heat down slightly and simmer until almost all of the balsamic vinegar has disappeared, about 8 minutes.

Stir in walnuts and continue stirring until they are well coated. Serve warm or at room temperature.

Macronutrient Profile (per serving)

	Grams	Calories	%-Cals
Calories		157	
Fat	13	110	72%
Saturated	1	10	7%
Polyunsaturated	9	79	52%
Monounsaturated	2	15	10%
Carbohydrate	8	32	21%
Dietary Fibre	2		
Protein	3	11	7%

DUKKAH

Time in the Kitchen: 10 minutes
Servings: 350 g (12 oz) *(macronutrient profile based on serving size of 2½ tablespoons)*

115 g (4 oz) hazelnuts
20 g (¾ oz) coriander seeds
2 tablespoons sesame seeds
2 tablespoons cumin seeds
1 teaspoon black peppercorns
1 teaspoon fennel seeds
½ teaspoon salt

Dukkah is an Egyptian blend of nuts and spices, often combined with olive oil. Dukkah is often served as a dip or spooned over cooked meat and vegetables. The combination of spices used for Dukkah varies according to who's making it. Give this blend a try, then make it your own by adding or eliminating spices and herbs and experimenting with different types of nuts.

Put all ingredients, except salt, in a pan over a medium heat and toast for two minutes.

Leave to cool then mix with salt and grind either in a food processor or with a pestle and mortar. The texture should be coarse, not as smooth as a paste. Can be stored in an airtight container for several weeks.

Macronutrient Profile (per serving)

	Grams	Calories	%-Cals
Calories		114	
Fat	10	82	72%
Saturated	1	7	6%
Polyunsaturated	2	14	13%
Monounsaturated	7	57	50%
Carbohydrate	7	20	18%
Dietary Fibre	5		
Protein	3	11	10%

CHILLI COCOA RUB

Time in the Kitchen: 5 minutes
Servings: Enough to season
at least 450 g (1 lb) of protein

1 tablespoon chilli powder
1 teaspoon cocoa powder
½ teaspoon cinnamon
¼ teaspoon nutmeg

The pleasantly bitter flavour of unsweetened chocolate and smoky flavour of chilli powder pairs best with barbecued or grilled steak.

Mix spices together and rub on meat before cooking.

JAMAICAN JERK RUB

Time in the Kitchen: 10 minutes
Servings: Enough to season
at least 450 g (1 lb) of protein

1 teaspoon dried thyme
1 teaspoon granulated garlic
½ teaspoon black pepper
¼ teaspoon allspice
¼ teaspoon dried onion
¼ teaspoon dried ginger
¼ teaspoon cinnamon
⅛ teaspoon nutmeg
⅛ teaspoon cayenne pepper

Jamaican rubs are fiery blends balanced with the sweetness that comes from baking spices like cinnamon, nutmeg and allspice. No two Jamaican Jerk rubs are the same and you can play around with the quantities of each spice to create your own perfect rub for pork or chicken.

Simply combine all the spices.

Quick & Easy Tip:

Salt is not included in most of the rub recipes, but does help bring out flavour. You can add a teaspoon of salt to any rub you make, or simply wait and salt the meat to taste after cooking.

FENNEL AND LEMON RUB

Time in the Kitchen: 5 minutes
Servings: Enough to season
at least 450 g (1 lb) of protein

1   tablespoon fennel seeds
1   teaspoon dried lemon peel
1   teaspoon dried parsley

Fennel seeds have a stronger flavour than fresh fennel but even so, those who profess not to like the flavour of liquorice shouldn't be scared away. The liquorice-like flavour of fennel seeds is not overpowering when mixed with dried lemon peel and parsley. These flavours are best with lamb and pork, or fish such as cod and halibut.

Grind fennel seeds in a coffee grinder or with a pestle and mortar and mix with parsley and lemon.

CORIANDER MUSTARD SEED RUB

Time in the Kitchen: 10 minutes
Servings: Enough to season
at least 900 g (2 lb) of protein

2   tablespoons coriander seeds
1   tablespoon cumin seeds
1   teaspoon mustard seeds
1   teaspoon green cardamom pods
1   teaspoon nutmeg

The flavour and aroma of coriander has a hint of lemon that blends in well with the stronger flavours and powerful aromatics of spices like cardamom and cumin. Try this rub with lamb or beef that is slowly cooked to tenderness.

In a frying pan over a medium heat, toast coriander, cumin, mustard, and cardamom for about 3 minutes. The spices will become more fragrant and slightly darker as they toast and some of the seeds might make popping noises.

Cool, then finely grind with remaining ingredients in a coffee grinder or with a pestle and mortar.

Quick & Easy Tip:

A pestle and mortar consists of a bowl and a rounded tool used to crush and grind ingredients. You can find a pestle and mortar at most kitchenware shops. To get the job done faster, dedicate a coffee grinder in your kitchen for only grinding spices.

GARLIC
LOVERS' RUB

Time in the Kitchen: 5 minutes
Servings: Enough to season
at least 450 g (1 lb) of protein

1 tablespoon granulated garlic
1 teaspoon black peppercorns
½ teaspoon cumin seeds
½ teaspoon onion powder

The name really says it all for this rub. Fresh garlic tends to burn and become bitter when heated for long periods of time, which is where dried garlic comes in handy. Use this rub on roasts that will be cooked for extended periods of time or meat that is cooked over a high heat.

Grind together garlic, peppercorns and cumin seeds in a coffee grinder or with a pestle and mortar. Mix with onion powder.

PEPPER
LOVERS' RUB

Time in the Kitchen: 5 minutes
Servings: Enough to season
at least 450 g (1 lb) of protein

1 tablespoon Sichuan
   peppercorns
1 teaspoon black peppercorns
½ teaspoon dried lemon peel

This rub has plenty of heat from the peppercorns, but spicy isn't all you get. Sichuan peppercorns have an earthy and lemony quality that really comes out when heated. Great on seafood, like prawns and squid, and on red meat.

Toast peppercorns in a pan over a medium heat for several minutes until lightly toasted and aromatic.

Grind in a coffee grinder or with a pestle and mortar and combine with lemon peel.

Quick & Easy Tip:

Dried lemon or orange peel can be found in the spice section of some markets. If you can't find it, make your own by using a paring knife to trim away just the coloured part of the lemon or orange skin with no white pith attached. Lay the strips skin-side down on a plate and let them dry for a few days until they shrivel and are no longer moist. To use, either crumble the dried peel or if you have enough, whirl it in a blender. Store in a covered jar.

MOROCCAN RUB

Time in the Kitchen: 5 minutes
Servings: Enough to season
at least 450 g (1 lb) of protein

1 tablespoon coriander seeds
1 teaspoon caraway seeds
½ teaspoon cinnamon
½ teaspoon allspice
¼ teaspoon chilli flakes

Spice combinations that are simultaneously earthy and sweet with just a bit of heat always bring to mind the complex flavours of Moroccan cuisine. This rub is especially good on lamb or pork.

Toast coriander and caraway seeds in a pan over a medium heat for several minutes.

Grind in a coffee grinder or with a pestle and mortar and mix with cinnamon, allspice and chilli flakes.

LAVENDER RUB

Time in the Kitchen: 5 minutes
Servings: Enough to season
at least 450 g (1 lb) of protein

1 tablespoon lavender buds
1 teaspoon dried parsley
1 teaspoon dried thyme
½ teaspoon fennel seeds

This rub is similar to *Herbes de Provence*, a mixture of dried herbs used in the cuisine of Southern France. Lavender does indeed bring a bit of a floral quality, but the parsley, thyme and fennel bring plenty of savoury flavour to balance it out. Chicken, lamb and roasted vegetables are especially good with this incredibly aromatic blend.

Buy dried lavender in the spice section of a speciality grocery store, market or online to ensure you are getting culinary-grade lavender. If harvesting your own lavender, make sure it's pesticide-free and a species of lavender that has a flavour suitable for eating.

Grind all ingredients together briefly in coffee grinder or with a pestle and mortar.

SESAME SEAWEED RUB

Time in the Kitchen: 5 minutes
Servings: Enough to season
at least 450 g (1 lb) of protein

2 tablespoons black sesame seeds
1 tablespoon dulse flakes
½ teaspoon salt

This rub can be added to seafood or red meat before cooking, but it's really better as a seasoning after the protein has been cooked. Shake onto salads and vegetables too, or blend with sesame oil for a quick dressing.

Dulse flakes are paper-thin slivers of dried seaweed. Often found in health food shops or speciality grocery stores, dulse has high amounts of magnesium and calcium.

Mix ingredients together. That's it!

GINGER RUB

Time in the Kitchen: 5 minutes
Servings: Enough to season
at least 450 g (1 lb) of protein

1 teaspoon ginger
⅛ teaspoon granulated garlic
1 teaspoon dried orange peel
¼ teaspoon Chinese five spice powder

Dried ginger tends to be spicier than the fresh root, so a little bit goes a long way. This warm and inviting spice blend is tastiest on red meat, but can also be used with duck or pork.

Simply mix spices together.

INDEX

scallops, 120, 124, 166
seaweed, 128, 222
sesame oil, 62, 68, 100, 118, 128, 170, 176, 192
sesame seeds, 62, 74, 128, 184, 210, 222
shallot, 40, 114, 122, 132, 134, 164, 188, 192, 196, 202, 206
sherry vinegar, 38, 40, 56, 72, 74, 76, 98, 154
shiitake mushrooms, 84, 128
Sichuan peppercorns, 218
sirloin, 78, 128
skirt steak, 34, 38, 78, 80, 134
smoked salmon, 36, 172
sour cream, 194
spaghetti squash, 26, 130
Spanish olives, 154
spinach, 28, 48, 92, 128, 200
spring onions, 42, 62, 72, 84, 90, 100, 118, 120, 128, 146, 170, 200
squash, 12
    spaghetti, 26, 130
squid, 168
steak, 30, 38, 100, 132
    flank, 34, 76, 78, 128
    skirt, 34, 38, 80, 134
    sirloin, 78, 128
stock
    beef, 46
    chicken, 46, 90, 108, 110, 120, 122, 124, 134, 198, 202
    fish, 124
    vegetable, 122
sultanas, 206
swedes, 160
sweet chilli sauce, 192

T

tahini, 68, 74
tamari, 68, 84, 100, 118, 128, 170, 176, 184
tarragon, 164
thyme, 154, 161, 214, 220
tomato, 20, 24, 30, 48, 80, 82, 88, 114, 124, 130, 168
    canned, 104, 110, 124
    cherry, 38
    paste, 14
tuna, 60

turmeric, 114
turnip, 42, 104, 134, 160

V

vanilla, 6, 8
vegetable stock, 122
vinegar
    apple cider, 16
    balsamic, 206, 208
    red wine, 76, 77
    rice wine, 62, 68, 70, 128, 170, 192
    sherry, 38, 40, 56, 72, 74, 76, 98, 154
    white wine, 16, 52, 122, 124

W

walnuts, 4, 6, 52, 70, 148, 152, 162, 196, 208
    oil, 52
watercress, 48, 164
white onion, 46, 80, 100, 104, 108, 124, 136
white wine, 52, 108, 122, 124
white wine vinegar, 16, 52, 122, 124

Y

yellow onion, 46, 100, 104, 124
yogurt, 16, 114

NOTES